CHARACTER COUNTS!

Benjamin Franklin: *"I would rather have it said, he lived usefully, than he died rich."*

Abraham Lincoln: *"Always bear in mind that your own resolution to succeed is more important than any other one thing."*

Theodore Roosevelt: *"It is not the critic who counts, not the man who points out how the strong man stumbles, or where the doer of deeds could have done better. The credit belongs to the man who is actually in the arena, whose face is marred by dust and sweat and blood; who strives valiantly; who errs, and comes short again and again, because there is not effort without error and shortcoming; but who does actually strive to do the deeds; who knows the great enthusiasms, the great devotions; who spends himself in a worthy cause."*

Comment on Calvin Coolidge: *"…people liked him because he kept his word and was scrupulously honest. He inherited from his Vermont ancestors their characteristics of plain living and high thinking, taciturnity and humor."*

Eleanor Roosevelt on husband Franklin: *"Remember, the nicest men in the world are those who always keep something of a little boy in them."*

Harry Truman: When asked if he was an 'average man', Truman replied *"Well, what is wrong with being an average man?"*

Gerald Ford: *"…there is no undertaking more challenging, no responsibility more awesome, than that of being a mother."*

Hear Ye! Hear Ye!

Wit *and* Wisdom *of*
★ ★ U.S. Presidents as ★ ★
Character Professors

James Martin Tervo

James Martin Tervo
Janet S. Burch
PO Box 47
The Sea Ranch, CA 95497

Copyright © 2023 by James Martin Tervo. All rights reserved. No part of this book may be reproduced in any form or by any means whatsoever without written permission of James Martin Tervo or Janet S. Burch.

ISBN 979-8-218-12745-9 (Hardcover)
ISBM 979-8-218-15615-2 (ebook)

Design: The Book Designers
Bookdesigners.com

Printed by: Edition One Books
Richmond, California
Editiononebooks.com

To my beautiful and thoughtful wife Janet.
Love you more.

TABLE *of* CONTENTS
OUR CHARACTER PROFESSORS

ix PROLOGUE........ Deceitful Presidential Character begets Deceitful Character of our Citizens, Especially our Youth

1 CHAPTER ONE............................. Godfather Benjamin Franklin
17 CHAPTER TWO............................ George Washington
31 CHAPTER THREE .... John Adams
45 CHAPTER FOUR........................... Thomas Jefferson
55 CHAPTER FIVE .... Abraham Lincoln
69 CHAPTER SIX .... Ulysses S. Grant
81 CHAPTER SEVEN .... Theodore Roosevelt
103 CHAPTER EIGHT....................... William Howard Taft
113 CHAPTER NINE........................ Woodrow Wilson
123 CHAPTER TEN........................... Calvin Coolidge
137 CHAPTER ELEVEN................... Herbert Hoover
149 CHAPTER TWELVE .... Franklin Delano Roosevelt
165 CHAPTER THIRTEEN .... Harry S. Truman
179 CHAPTER FOURTEEN .... Dwight D. Eisenhower
195 CHAPTER FIFTEEN .... Gerald R. Ford
209 CHAPTER SIXTEEN .... Personal Reflections

223 NOTES
239 ILLUSTRATION LIST AND CREDITS
242 ABOUT THE AUTHOR

Eisenhower, Patton and Truman in Berlin 1945

Taft and T. Roosevelt at Taft's Inaugural 1909

PROLOGUE

DECEITFUL PRESIDENTIAL CHARACTER BEGETS DECEITFUL CHARACTER OF OUR CITIZENS, ESPECIALLY OUR YOUTH

During my lifetime, our American presidents have been chosen, perhaps properly so, based on political ideology more so than their personal character values. The result is we have not always elected a person with sterling personal values.

This raises the basic question – Does character count in our elected officials? In our neighbors? In our colleagues at work? Do Americans continue to instill in their children the personal character values that have been a cornerstone of our American heritage and culture?

Renowned author and historian Robert Dallek, in the preface to his 2017 biography *Franklin D. Roosevelt, A Political Life*, discusses the current cynical attitude of many Americans toward politicians because of the belief politicians are primarily out for themselves, and act at times less than honorably. He is especially concerned with the negative impact on the values of America's youth brought about by our elected officials acting dishonorably. He writes,

"Every scandal or hint of malfeasance only deepens that conviction…In 2016 national cynicism expressed itself in an initial low turnout at the polls. Only 9 percent of potential *voters participated in both parties' primary elections. Distrust of the 2016 Presidential aspirants, Republican Donald Trump and Democrat Hillary Clinton, marked a surge of disgust about the parties and their chiefs that raised doubts about the genius of American politics."*[1]

Dallek goes on to describe one of his principal motivations for writing his biography on FDR:

"It seems well, then, despite the large body of fine existing biographies, histories and documentary collections, to remind people, especially a younger generation with limited knowledge of American history, of what great presidential leadership looks like."[2]

Mr. Dallek labels the present era as "this time of demoralization."

The presidential and many congressional elections of 2020 continued to exhibit the voters neglect of character values of the candidates, and reinforced the cynical attitudes of many Americans toward would-be leaders of our country. The January 6, 2021 insurrection at the U.S. Capitol was a poor demonstration of the American character. Sadly, at times our American youth must wonder about the importance of their own personal character values.

President Nixon on the Watergate burglary:

"I can say categorically that…no one in the White House staff, no one in this administration, presently employed, was involved in this very bizarre incident."[3]

President Reagan on the Iran-Contra scandal:

"In spite of the wildly speculative and false stories of arms for

hostages and alleged ransom payments, we did not, repeat, did not, trade weapons or anything else for hostages. Nor will we."[4]

President George W. Bush on weapons of mass destruction:
"We found weapons of mass destruction [in Iraq]. We found biological laboratories."[5]

President Lyndon Johnson on the Vietnam War:
"We are not about to send American boys nine or ten thousand miles away from home to do what Asian boys ought to be doing for themselves."[6]

President Bill Clinton on his affair with White House intern Monica Lewinsky:
"I did not have sexual relations with that woman, Ms. Lewinsky. I never told anybody to lie, not a single time, never."[7]

President Trump on January 6, 2021 on the Ellipse outside the White House prior to the ransacking of the Capitol:
"We won this election, and we won it by a landslide. This was not a close election."[8]

    I echo Mr. Dallek's concerns on the effects of questionable character values of our leaders on the youth of America. Deceitful character begets deceitful character. Perhaps in some small way this book, by shining the light on some of the positive personal values of previous great American leaders, might offset "this time of demoralization."
    Our country began on a solid foundation thanks to the remarkable personal qualities of many of our Founding Fathers. Subsequent to our Founding Fathers we also have been blessed with many quality people who became president;

men with ideals and virtues to be emulated. Two of these are Abraham Lincoln and Gerald Ford:

Jesse W. Fell, a friend of Abraham Lincoln, wrote,
> *"If there were any traits of character that stood out in bold relief, in the person of Mr. Lincoln, it was that of Truth and Candor. He was utterly incapable of insincerity…In the grand review of his peculiar characteristics, nothing creates such an impressive effect as his love of the truth."* [9]

Gerald Ford stated,
> *"I do not think a President under any circumstances that I can envision ought to lie to the American people."* [10]

Unfortunately it seems that the personal character attributes of these exceptional past presidents have generally been forgotten other than by a small number of historians and history buffs.

I have always been interested in American history and the men who have been our presidents. Probably similar to most Americans, I knew a few truths about the most well known presidents, but I wasn't confident of what was fact and what was myth. This book is the result of my curiosity of character.

My assumption is that we all (especially our youth) can benefit from a few meaningful reminders and examples of character values to be followed.

Keep in mind that the focus of this book is wit and wisdom on character, and not on successes or failures as president (upon which, of course, there are already a multitude of books and materials). I have ordained each president with a full "Professorship of Character" to reflect their new role as teacher and mentor.

Prologue

In discussing character, it is impossible not to mix in personality, and hobbies too. One cannot write about Eisenhower and not mention golf, or write about Truman and not mention "poker with the boys."

I have chosen fourteen past presidents plus Founding Father Benjamin Franklin (whom I call "America's Godfather") for inclusion in the following chapters, spanning some two hundred years of our American heritage.

In Chapter Sixteen I will list a few of my favorite Red White and Blue Character Gems for special highlight. Also I have selected four of the men for my personal "Character Mount Rushmore."

Franklin, 1783, painting by Joseph-Siffred Duplessis

CHAPTER ONE

PERSONAL CHARACTER
VALUES OF CHARACTER
PROFESSOR BENJAMIN FRANKLIN
(1706 – 1790)

AMERICA'S GODFATHER *and* POSSIBLY AMERICA'S MOST INTERESTING MAN

"Be at war with your vices, at peace with your neighbors, and let every new year find you a better man."[1]
—BENJAMIN FRANKLIN

"I would rather have it said, he lived usefully, than he died rich."[2]
—BENJAMIN FRANKLIN

"I regard the reading of Franklin's Autobiography as the turning point of my life. Here was Franklin, poorer than myself, who by industry, thrift and frugality had become learned and wise, and elevated to wealth and fame…the maxims of 'Poor Richard' exactly suited my sentiments."[3]
—THE INDUSTRIALIST AND BANKER THOMAS MELLON

I call Ben Franklin the Godfather of our country. Franklin was twenty-six years older than George Washington and was eighty-three when Washington became president. No Founding Father, except George Washington, contributed more to our independence and formation of our country than Franklin. He is the only person to negotiate and sign all four of the most important documents of his era:

(i) *The Declaration of Independence;*

(ii) *The Franco-American Treaty of Alliance and Commerce that brought France into the Revolutionary War (called by one historian "the greatest diplomatic victory the United States ever achieved");*

(iii) *The Treaty of Paris, the peace treaty with Britain ending the Revolutionary War, and*

(iv) *The U.S. Constitution.*

During his life he was the most famous man in America, if not the world. He was a printer, publisher, author, postmaster, civic leader, scientist, inventor, politician, political theorist, and international diplomat.

It is fortuitous that we start with Franklin because of the fifteen people we are going to discuss, Franklin wrote the most extensively of all about the importance of one's personal character values.

FAMILY BACKGROUND *and* INFLUENCES ON FRANLKIN'S CHARACTER

Ben was born into poverty in Boston in 1706 to parents of English Puritan heritage. He was the fifteenth of seventeen children of his father Josiah, who was a candle and soap maker. Ben had only two years of schooling. At the age of twelve he was apprenticed to his older brother James under a nine-year contract. James was a printer and newspaper publisher in Boston. At age sixteen Ben started writing anonymously satirical essays for his brother's newspaper. His brother was abusive and at age seventeen Ben ran away to Philadelphia, alone and with no money. He found work assisting a printer and not long after started his own printing and publishing business. His business flourished and Ben became wealthy, especially from his annual publishing of *Poor Richard's Almanac* of which he was the author. Independently wealthy, he retired in his late 40's and devoted the remainder of his life to public service and his scientific research and experiments.

In 1730 when Ben was twenty-five he entered into a common law (no license, no ceremony) marriage with Deborah Reed (1708-1774). Deborah worked in the printing business, helped it succeed, and she was frugal like Ben. Ben and Deborah had two children, Francis who died at age four from smallpox and Sally (1743-1808), who married businessman Richard Bache, had seven children and looked after Ben in his final years.

Ben moved to London in 1757 as a diplomatic envoy for Pennsylvania. In late 1776 as the envoy to France, Ben moved to a small village outside Paris, where he remained for eight years. He lived twenty-three of his last thirty years in Europe. While in Europe, Ben was a world celebrity and hosted a constant stream of visitors. The great statesmen, scientists and philosophers of Europe came to meet him.

HEAR YE! HEAR YE!

CHARACTER PROFESSOR FRANKLIN'S RED WHITE *and* BLUE CHARACTER GEMS

Franklin's Character Gem No. 1

REGARDLESS OF YOUR BACKGROUND, IN AMERICA OPPORTUNITY EXISTS IF YOU ARE INDUSTRIOUS AND FRUGAL.

Ben wrote:

"Energy and persistence conquer all things."[4]

Franklin is the quintessential example of a self-made man, rising from poverty and lack of formal schooling to become independently wealthy and retiring at age forty-two. His wealth came solely from his printing and publishing business which he started alone from scratch. He emphatically believed that America was the land of opportunity where one, regardless of origin or social class, could achieve upward economic mobility.

Regarding frugality, Ben said:

"When you run in debt, you give another power over your liberty."[5]

"He that goes a-borrowing, goes a-sorrowing."[6]

Franklin's American Character Gem No. 2
SMILE, PUT A TWINKLE IN YOUR EYE.

Franklin was a "people person" in an unaggressive, charming "twinkle in his eye" low key way. He smiled and was good natured, "up" and at ease with people he met, frequently using humor to enrich a conversation. At a young age, Franklin realized that success was more easily obtainable with help from superiors and patrons who took a liking to him. He spoke ill of no one and each person he met he considered to be an asset. People enjoyed his companionship, respected him and the result was that folks helped him obtain his goals, whether it be in his printing business or as a diplomat and negotiator in Europe.

Franklin's Character Gem No. 3
YOU LIVE HAPPIER AND YOU BENEFIT BY BEING VIRTUOUS.

Franklin resolved to always do the correct thing and to avoid wrongdoing. He felt this would lead to a happy peaceful life and also lead to better social and business relations. At age twenty he wrote down thirteen virtues to follow and then devised a methodology to assist him to help him comply. He created a chart with thirteen rows and seven columns, one for each day of the week. He would work on one virtue each week, check the appropriate box, and go through the thirteen virtues four times a year (13 x 4 = 52 weeks). Franklin's thirteen virtues, which have been repeatedly published worldwide:

(1) *Temperance.* Eat not to dullness; drink not to elevation.

(2) *Silence.* Speak not but what may benefit others or yourself; avoid trifling conversation.

(3) *Order.* Let all your things have their places; let each part of your business have its time.

(4) *Resolution.* Resolve to perform what you ought; perform without fail what you resolve.

(5) *Frugality.* Make no expense but to do good to others or yourself; i.e. waste nothing.

(6) *Industry.* Lose no time; be always employed in something useful; cut off all unnecessary actions.

(7) *Sincerity.* Use no hurtful deceit; think innocently and justly, and if you speak, speak accordingly.

(8) *Justice.* Wrong none by doing injuries, or omitting the benefits that are your duty.

(9) *Moderation.* Avoid extremes; forbear resenting injuries so much as you think they deserve.

(10) *Cleanliness.* Tolerate no uncleanliness in body, clothes, or habitation.

(11) *Tranquility.* Be not disturbed at trifles, or at accidents common or unavoidable.

(12) *Chastity.* Rarely use venery but for health or offspring, never to dullness, weakness, or the injury of your own or another's peace or reputation.

(13) *Humility.* Imitate Jesus and Socrates.[7]

At age seventy-nine Ben admitted he never completely mastered the thirteen virtues, but knew he was a better and happier man for attempting:

"Tho' I never arrived at the perfection I had been so ambitious of obtaining but fell short of it, yet I was, by endeavor, a better and happier man than I otherwise should have been if I had not attempted it."[8]

Franklin's Character Gem No. 4

LEARN YOUR STRENGTHS AND WEAKNESSES, AND THEN EMBARK ON A SELF-IMPROVEMENT PLAN OF YOUR OWN DESIGN, NO MATTER WHAT YOUR AGE.

Franklin looked introspectively and examined his strengths and weaknesses. He understood how difficult it was to know yourself:

"There are three things extremely hard: steel, a diamond, and to know one's self."[9]

"Search others for their virtues, thy self for thy vices."[10]

He encouraged others to follow his example and write out a self-improvement plan. He believed at every age there is room for improvement. He carried a small notebook which contained his personal thirteen virtues and his corresponding compliance chart throughout his lifetime. Even in his late 70's, he proudly showed the notebook to the French while living outside Paris.

"Some people die at 25 and are buried at 75."[11]

"When you're finished changing, you're finished."[12]

Franklin's Character Gem No. 5
AVOID DIRECT CONFRONTATION WITH OTHERS.

Ben wrote:

"What begins in anger ends in shame."[13]

Franklin taught himself to never argue or directly contradict anyone. He developed a gentle indirect style of discussion and debate. He wrote,

"Would you win the hearts of others, you must not seem to vie with them, but to admire them."[14]

"Those disputing, contradicting, and confuting people are generally unfortunate in their affairs. They get victory, sometimes, but they never get good will, which would be of more use to them."[15]

Franklin's Character Gem No. 6
MONEY IS A MEANS AND NOT THE END GOAL.

Franklin's passion for frugality shouldn't be misunderstood. His goal was not the accumulation of wealth. Rather, money was to be accumulated in order to be a useful tool.

Franklin wrote:

"To pour forth benefits to the common good is divine."[16]

Franklin retired from business at age forty-two to concentrate on his inventions and public service. Accumulating more money was no longer necessary or of interest. He declined lucrative patent rights on his inventions such as his stove. His inventions were to benefit society, not him personally.

He was a major philanthropist. The citizens of his beloved Philadelphia were the main beneficiaries and Franklin was behind virtually every scheme that made Philadelphia an attractive place to live. His wealth helped make these initiatives possible. He funded any religious denomination that requested assistance and it is said that he contributed to the building fund of every church, temple and synagogue in Philadelphia.

Franklin's Character Gem No. 7

SHAPE AND ALWAYS PROTECT YOUR PUBLIC IMAGE.

Franklin knew a person's public image and reputation were extremely important for success.

Some historians suggest Franklin was America's first public relations expert. Franklin was sensitive to his image when he was building his printing business and felt it was essential to not only *be* industrious and frugal, but also *appear* to be industrious and frugal. There are stories of him pushing his wheel barrow down Market Street in Philadelphia to create a lasting impression on others.

Franklin successfully re-crafted his public persona at times if he felt it beneficial. In France as a diplomat and negotiator on behalf of America, he created the persona of an American frontier philosopher and intellect by wearing plain clothes, a coonskin cap and spectacles. It must have worked as Yale historian and biographer, Edmund Morgan, called the Franco-American Treaty of Alliance bringing French troops and needed funds into the Revolutionary War,

"the greatest diplomatic victory the U.S. has ever achieved."[17]

Franklin also knew one screw-up can quickly ruin a reputation:

"It takes many good deeds to build a good reputation, and only one bad one to lose it."[18]

Franklin's Character Gem No. 8
HOORAY FOR THE VALUES OF AMERICA'S WORKING MIDDLE CLASS.

Ben's ideal were the shopkeepers, the "middling class" as he called them, who were industrious and self-reliant.

Franklin's Character Gem No. 9
BE PRACTICAL AND BE WILLING TO COMPROMISE.

The terms "practical" and "compromise" define Ben's approach to his business, his scientific research, his local civic volunteerism, and his diplomatic and governmental service. Being practical and working with clients made him wealthy. Being practical, compromising and building consensus amongst various self-interests allowed him to successfully bring people together for his civic improvement projects.

Ben was intellectually curious, but his scientific research was followed by practical application for society's benefit; i.e. swim fins and bifocals. After proving lightning was electricity, Ben developed lightning rods to protect buildings and homes. He achieved spectacular success as a diplomat because he was able to compromise and blend ideals with reality. At the Constitutional Convention, he played the role of a practical conciliator, the compromiser who helped draft the modifications which allowed the big states and small states to reach an acceptable result.

Franklin's Character Gem No. 10
DO VOLUNTEER WORK AND SUPPORT YOUR LOCAL CIVIC AND CHARITABLE ORGANIZATIONS.

Franklin's passion for improvement didn't stop at personal self-improvement. He was passionate about improving his community through his practical inventions and through formation and support of community improvement organizations, such as a public library, fire department, hospital, and the University of Pennsylvania. It is joked that Franklin is the "Father of all Kiwanians." Ben saw the potential strength of people collaborating through clubs and associations for mutual benefit. He wrote:

"The good men may do separately is small compared to what they may do collectively."[19]

Franklin's Character Gem No. 11
IMPORTANCE OF TIME MANAGEMENT.

For every day, Franklin wrote out a time schedule. Time management was one of his passions and he thought less of people that misused their time or misused his.

"You may delay, but time will not, and lost time is never found again."[20]

Franklin's Character Gem No. 12
BE (OR AT LEAST ACT!) HUMBLE.

Franklin admitted that for him the most difficult of his thirteen virtues (listed above in Gem No. 3) was humility. Although Ben's nature was such that he never put on fancy airs and he treated everyone as an equal, he definitely felt pride of his accomplishments and the accolades. He suppressed his ego and went out of his way to share credit with others for any successes.

"The present little sacrifice of your vanity will afterwards be aptly repaid."[21]

In writing about his struggle with the virtue of humility,

"Disguise it, struggle with it, beat it down, stifle it, mortify it as much as one pleases, it is still alive and will every now and then peep out and show itself."[22]

Franklin's Character Gem No. 13
PROACTIVELY SUPPORT INDIVIDUAL RIGHTS.

Franklin never thought he was better than anyone else and treated everyone equally. His religious views were based on doing good deeds for others, rather than salvation from beliefs. He made significant charitable contributions to various diverse religious groups.

In 1787 at age eighty Ben became an outspoken abolitionist and president of the Pennsylvania Society for Promoting the Abolition of Slavery, which was organized by the Pennsylvania Quakers. In 1790 he petitioned Congress on behalf of the Society to abolish slavery. At the time this was a radical position that was highly criticized by many. Today historians have uniformly praised Franklin for his acts of courage, although late in life.

Franklin's Character Gem No. 14
ENJOY A GLASS OR TWO OF WINE (BUT BEWARE THE GOUT!).

Although Ben's first of his thirteen virtues is temperance and although he suffered from gout, he did enjoy a glass of wine. Ben is widely credited with saying,

"Wine is the constant proof that God loves us and wants to see us happy."[23]

However he also reminds us,

"When wine enters, out goes the truth."[24]

Franklin's Character Gem No. 15
LISTEN AND LEARN.

"More is to be learned with the ear than the tongue."[25]

Franklin's Character Gem No. 16
IF POSSIBLE, LIVE ABROAD FOR A PERIOD OF TIME.

Franklin lived in England and France for twenty-three years.

Franklin's Character Gem No. 17
CULTIVATE AND ENJOY HOBBIES.

Franklin enjoyed scientific tinkering and experimenting, reading and writing, humor, swimming, chess and socializing with friends.

Washington, 1795, painting by Rembrandt Peale

CHAPTER TWO

PERSONAL CHARACTER VALUES OF PRESIDENT AND CHARACTER PROFESSOR GEORGE WASHINGTON
(1732 - 1799)
(1st U.S. President 1789 - 1797)

ARDENT REVOLUTIONARY *who* DEDICATED HIS LIFE *TO* WINNING *the* REVOLUTIONARY WAR *and then* NATION BUILDING TRULY FATHER OF OUR COUNTRY

"On the whole, his [Washington's] character was, in its mass, perfect…and it may truly be said, that never did nature and fortune combine more perfectly to make a great man."[1]

—THOMAS JEFFERSON,
later to be Washington's bitter political opponent

Washington, 1772, painting by Charles Willson Peale

No Founding Father sacrificed more than George Washington for victory in the Revolutionary War, having served as Commander-in-Chief of the Continental Army for eight and a half years, enduring hardship and misery. Then only a few years after the war he was recalled to public service from his idyllic Mount Vernon to be America's first president. Many historians believe Washington was our greatest president:

> "...the movement that Washington found himself heading was also the most consequential event in American history, the crucible within which the political personality of the United States took shape. In effect, the character of the man and the character of the nation congealed and grew together during an extended moment of eight years."[2]

Washington, as was true for Ben Franklin, offers us a wealth of Red White and Blue Character Gems. Washington and Franklin were considerably different people and used differing styles to become leaders and achieve successes. Franklin wore a smile, was easy going, approachable, and used humor and wit in his conversations. People enjoyed his company and wanted to support his many projects. Washington had a majestic, awe inspiring presence, and was more stern, distant and less approachable. He inspired trust and confidence, and people wanted him to be their leader and they would follow his command. Interestingly, both used clothes to mold their image. Franklin dressed down more often than not, including when he went to Versailles to dine with King Louis XVI and Queen Marie Antoinette. Franklin wanted to mold an image of an American backwoods intellectual. Washington was the opposite, dressing immaculately in high fashion to mold an image of power and authority.

FAMILY BACKGROUND *and* INFLUENCES *on* WASHINGTON'S CHARACTER

George Washington was born in 1732 in rural Virginia to parents of English descent, Augustine and Mary Washington. Augustine was a successful farmer and businessman. He had ten children, four with his first wife and then six with Mary. Augustine died when George was eleven. Augustine and George were not close, in part because Augustine traveled much of the time on business. George's mother Mary was said to be headstrong and stubborn and George received little maternal warmth.

George had no formal schooling past the age of fifteen. At age sixteen in 1748 he began his career as a surveyor. This was interrupted when he became an officer in the colonial militia during the French and Indian War (1753-1758). In 1759 he married wealthy widow Martha Dandridge Custis which elevated George to the top of Virginia society. He had previously inherited Mount Vernon from his half-brother, but with Martha's wealth George became an independently wealthy gentleman farmer. George was a faithful husband and they shared a warm affectionate marriage. George and Martha had no children of their own but George was a dutiful stepfather to Martha's two children.

CHARACTER PROFESSOR WASHINGTON'S RED WHITE *and* BLUE CHARACTER GEMS

Washington's Character Gem No. 1

IT'S REPUTATION, REPUTATION, REPUTATION! PROACTIVELY MOLD AND PROTECT YOUR REPUTATION.

The driving force in Washington's life was his passion to establish his reputation. To Washington, reputation was the measure of one's worth. His challenge was that he started his adult life as a poorly educated outdoorsman. Then in 1759 at age twenty-seven, he married a wealthy widow and leaped into the highest level of Virginia society. He understood his background and its deficiencies, but through determination he successfully took steps to mold his persona and put himself in situations where he could do great things.

As history professor Bill Abbot put it,

"Washington's biography is the story of a man constructing himself."[3]

After the Revolutionary War, Washington was one of the world's most famous person, yet he still worried that by accepting further public service positions he might fail and do significant harm to his stellar reputation.

Washington's Character Gem No. 2
CONTROL YOUR TEMPER.

Washington had a volcanic temper, but through grit and determination was able to essentially master control over it. As mentioned in Washington's Character Gem No. 1, Washington's life story is that of a man constructing himself, and controlling his temper was an important part of this. Founding Father Gouverneur Morris reflected on Washington's temper:

"…Washington's legendary calmness and statue-like stolidity masked truly volcanic energies and emotions. Any who knew him will bear witness that his wrath was terrible."[4]

Washington's Character Gem No. 3
YOU ARE DEFINED BY YOUR INTEGRITY AND YOUR MORAL AND ETHICAL STANDARDS.

Flawless character values established Washington's reputation and defined who he was. Alexander Hamilton regarded Washington as a man of unimpeachable integrity who would,

"never yield to any dishonorable or disloyal plans."[5]

Washington was never disingenuous and legitimately always tried to do the right thing. James Madison wrote that Washington was…

"The last man in the world to whom any measure whatever of deceptive tendency could be creditably attended."[6]

Thomas Jefferson wrote,

"His integrity was most pure, his justice the most inflexible I have ever known. No motives of interest or consanguinity, of friendship, or hatred, being able to bias his decisions."[7]

Washington's Character Gem No. 4
ENJOY A RURAL LIFESTYLE.

Washington preferred to be a gentleman farmer at his rural Mount Vernon home, as opposed to city living. He returned to Mount Vernon immediately at the conclusion of each pubic service tenure. There, on a regular basis, he was up at 5 a.m. and in the saddle for five to six hours managing the farmlands.

Washington's Character Gem No. 5
BE RESILIENT! BOUNCE BACK AND OVERCOME CHALLENGES AND HARDSHIPS.

Washington's inner strength and will power gave him the courage and stamina to overcome the miserable living conditions during the war and to overcome other life challenges. He had patience to stay the course. He acted upbeat and positive. He was depressed at times but not defeated. While at Valley Forge,

"I have no doubt that everything happens so far for the best; that we shall triumph over all our misfortunes and shall in the end be ultimately happy."[8]

Washington's Character Gem No. 6

BE A CAUTIOUS, THOROUGH, METHODICAL DECISION MAKER.

In making decisions, Washington was cautious and not impulsive, but once a decision was made, he proceeded forcefully. He was open to advice from others. He compromised and was conciliatory by nature. One colleague described his style,

"…no harum-scarum, ranting, swearing fellow, but sober, steady and calm."[9]

Thomas Jefferson, on Washington,

"Perhaps the strongest feature in his character was prudence, never acting until every circumstance, every consideration, was maturely weighed…"[10]

Washington's Character Gem No. 7

APPRECIATE THE IMPORTANCE OF APPEARANCE AND MANNERS.

Washington became passionate about having a dignified appearance. He dressed immaculately. He maintained perfect posture. It was said he had a graceful and dignified walk and gestures and near perfect manners. He never allowed people to see him in a casual, sloppy, disheveled way.

"Washington's devotion to courtesy and manners undoubtedly contributed to the social success of this reserved man."[11]

Washington's Character Gem No. 8
BE CHARITABLE, ESPECIALLY TO CHILDREN WITH NEEDS.

Washington gave money to educate numerous children of relatives and friends. He and Martha took in and raised orphans of extended family relatives. They always gave something to the numerous veterans, beggars and others that came by Mount Vernon. Washington to his grandson,

"Never let an indigent person ask without receiving something, if you have the means."[12]

Washington's Character Gem No. 9
HAVE COURAGE AND INNER STRENGTH!

Washington in the French and Indian War and again in the Revolutionary War repeatedly put himself in harm's way and showed courage under fire. He was a general who commanded from the front lines. His troops respected him for not asking them to do anything he wouldn't do.

Washington's Character Gem No. 10
VOLUNTEER, GIVE BACK TO THE COMMUNITY.

Washington had a strong sense of duty, of responsibility. He repeatedly agreed to serve the public, leaving Mount Vernon and sacrificing the quality of life for he and Martha.

Washington:

"That an army should sometimes be five or six days together without bread, then as many without meat, and once or twice two or three without either; that the same army should have had numbers of men in it with scarcely clothes enough to cover their nakedness and a full fourth of it without even the shadow of a blanket, severe as the winter was, and that men under these circumstances were held together, is hardly within the bounds of credibility, but is nevertheless true."[13]

Ron Chernow in his biography *Washington, A Life*:

"Seldom in history has a general been handicapped by such constantly crippling conditions. There was scarcely a time during the war when Washington didn't grapple with a crisis that threatened to disband the army and abort the Revolution. The extraordinary, wearisome, nerve-racking frustration he put up with for nearly nine years is hard to express. He repeatedly had to exhort Congress and the thirteen states to remedy desperate shortages of men, shoes, shirts, blankets and gunpowder. This meant dealing with selfish, apathetic states and bureaucratic incompetence in Congress. He labored under a terrible strain that would have destroyed a lesser man. Ennobled by adversity and leading by example, he had been dismayed and depressed but never defeated."[14]

Washington's Character Gem No. 11
KNOW WHEN TO GET OUT OF THE WAY AND PASS THE BATON TO ANOTHER.

At the end of the Revolutionary War, Washington was the most famous man in the world. Almost unprecedently, he then retired and gave up his power and authority, contrary to Caesar, Cromwell, Napoleon, Lenin and Mao, who parlayed their fame and position into wealth and continuing power. Historian Gordon S. Wood believes,

"The greatest act of his life, the one that gave him his greatest fame, was his resignation as Commander-in-Chief of the American forces."[15]

Other historians point to his refusal to accept a third presidential term as his most important act, in that it solidified America as a democracy.

Washington's Character Gem No. 12
BE MODEST.

Washington was not arrogant or bombastic.

Abigail Adams remarked,

"modesty marks every line and feature of his face."[16]

Washington's Character Gem No. 13
BEING PRACTICAL IS MORE IMPORTANT THAN BEING IDEALISTIC OR AN IDEOLOGUE.

Washington learned through experience. He was not in any way an intellectual who relished ideas for their own sake.

Washington's Character Gem No. 14
CULTIVATE AND ENJOY HOBBIES.

Washington enjoyed horses, hunting, dancing, card playing and dogs; he was uncomfortable making speeches.

Adams, between 1800-1815, painting by Gilbert Stuart

CHAPTER THREE

PERSONAL CHARACTER VALUES OF PRESIDENT AND CHARACTER PROFESSOR JOHN ADAMS
(1735-1826)
(2nd U.S. President 1797-1801)

PERHAPS *the* MOST INFLUENTIAL THINKER *and* ORATOR *of the* FOUNDING FATHERS, BUT *with a* PRICKLY PERSONALITY

"This illustrious patriot has not his superior, scarcely his equal for abilities and virtue on the whole of the continent of America."[1]
—FOUNDING FATHER DR. BENJAMIN RUSH
on John Adams

Abigail Adams, 1766, painting by Benjamin Blyth

George Washington was a significantly different person from Benjamin Franklin, and John Adams was significantly different from both Franklin and Washington. Unlike Franklin and Washington, Adams was argumentative and sarcastic to a fault. He was egotistical and intolerant of most folks. He was jealous of the fame and accolades given to Franklin, Washington and Jefferson and this led him to brooding, self-pity and despair.

Yet for all of the shortcomings of his personality, Adams was a giant of a man when it came to leading the colonies fight for independence and subsequent nation building. He sacrificed, took risks and worked tirelessly for the Revolutionary cause. He was a fiery bulldog who earned everyone's praise.

Equally important Adams led a family oriented and virtuous life, at all times with honor, truthfulness and integrity. Adams and wife Abagail had a true love affair. They exchanged over one thousand letters and theirs is one of the most famous marriages in American history.

FAMILY BACKGROUND *and* INFLUENCES *on* ADAMS' CHARACTER

John Adams was raised in Braintree (subsequently named Quincy), Massachusetts, in a humble lower middle class Puritan household of strict discipline. He both loved and idolized his father, John Sr., who was a farmer, local elected official and a deacon in their church. John also loved his mother, Susanna Boyston Adams, who was probably illiterate but came from a socially more prominent and well-to-do family than her husband. She was serious and strong-willed, with a temper.

Father John wanted his son to be a minister and so sent him to Boston to study at Harvard.

Upon graduation John chose instead to teach school during the day and study law in the evenings, passing the Massachusetts Bar in 1758. He practiced law in Braintree and then moved back to Boston, gaining respect from others for his lawyering skills, especially after his unpopular representation of eight British soldiers who had killed several Americans during the Boston Massacre. Six of the soldiers were acquitted. In the early 1770's John became increasingly more politically active and spent most of the balance of his life in public service. Not coming from a wealthy family, John's rise in prominence, capped off with becoming the second U.S. president, was solely the result of merit, i.e., intelligence, education and hard work.

In 1764 John married Abigail Smith (1744-1818), the daughter of a Congregational minister. It was the most significant and fortunate event in his life. They had a loving and happy marriage, and five children including John Quincy Adams who became the sixth U.S. president. As a result of John's many years of public service, John and Abigail never obtained wealth nor were considered part of Massachusetts' social elite. Abigail was an early advocate for equal rights for women,

> *"Remember the ladies and be more generous and favorable to them than your ancestors," she wrote to John. "Do not put such power into the hands of the Husbands. Remember all Men would be tyrants."*[2]

John never owned a slave, for reasons of principle, the opposite of numerous other Founding Fathers.

CHARACTER PROFESSOR ADAMS' RED WHITE *and* BLUE CHARACTER GEMS

Adams' Character Gem No. 1
A SPOUSE BRINGS HAPPINESS AND IS THE FOUNDATION FOR ALL ELSE IN LIFE.

Abigail was the core foundation of Adams' life, around which everything revolved. She was his love, best friend, confidante and equal intellectual partner.

"When he is wounded, I bleed,"[3] Abigail in 1781, their 17th year of marriage.

"I must go to you or you must come to me. I cannot live without you,"[4] Adams in 1797, their 33rd year of marriage.

When someone would compliment Adams on the career of his son, John Quincy Adams, he often would reply,

"My son had a mother."[5]

Adams' Character Gem No. 2
FIGHT FOR WHAT'S RIGHT! BE YOUR OWN PERSON, STUBBORNLY DEFEND YOUR OPINIONS AND DON'T WORRY ABOUT BEING "POPULAR."

Adams was a man of principles. Adams always said and acted as he felt. He never backed down or hid his opinions. He was frank and direct in conversation and was perceived at times as discourteous and overly argumentative.

"Popularity was never my mistress, nor was I ever, or shall I ever be a popular man."[6]

"Thanks to God that he gave me stubbornness when I know I am right."[7]

As Dr. Benjamin Rush observed, Adams was,

"…fearless of men and the consequences of a bold assertion of his opinion."[8]

Adams' Character Gem No. 3

TELL PEOPLE WHAT THEY NEED TO KNOW, EVEN IF IT ISN'T WHAT THEY WANT TO HEAR.

Adams coldly faced reality and told people what they needed to know. Adams famously said,

"Facts are stubborn things; and whatever may be our wishes, our inclinations, or the dictates of our passion, they cannot alter the state of facts and evidence."[9]

"…a man must be sensible of the errors of the people…and must run the risk of their displeasure sometimes, or he will never do them any good in the long run."[10]

Adams' Character Gem No. 4
LOVE YOUR FATHER.

His father was Adams' idol. His father was,

"the honestest man…in wisdom, piety, benevolence and charity in proportion to his education and sphere of life, I have never known his superior."[11]

Adams' Character Gem No. 5
ENJOY MILK AND VEGETABLES.

He believed milk and vegetables were crucial to a healthy diet,

"with very little animal food and still less spirituous liquors."[12]

He did enjoy hard cider and a little madeira wine.

Adams' Character Gem No. 6
IN MARRIAGE, LOOK FOR CHARACTER ABOVE ALL ELSE.

Adams' advice to his daughter,

"Daughter! … regard the honor and moral character of the man more than all other circumstances. An honest, sensible, humane man…laboring to do good rather than be rich, to be useful rather than make a show, living in modest simplicity clearly within his means and free from debts and obligations, is really the most respectable man in society, makes himself and all about him most happy."[13]

Adams' Character Gem No. 7

HAVE A PLAN! BE A THINKER, A PLANNER AND HAVE VISION OF THE FUTURE.

Part of Adams' genius and success is attributable to his ability to recognize the future, or at least the possibilities that lay ahead, and then to think and properly plan. Having a game plan was key. He knew where he wanted to take the colonies and then he planned and acted on his plans.

Adams' Character Gem No. 8

STRIVE TO EARN THE RESPECT OF OTHERS.

As was true for Washington, Adams felt a person's reputation is the be-all, end-all. Adams was driven to succeed and to accomplish great deeds by his fervent desire for respect and recognition. Adams,

"Reputation ought to be the perpetual subject of my Thoughts, and aim of my Behavior."[14]

Benjamin Rush commenting to Adams,

"You stand nearly alone in the history of our public in having never had your integrity called into question or even suspected…"[15]

Adams' Character Gem No. 9

APPRECIATE VOCABULARY AND THE MANNER OF EXPRESSION OF THOUGHTS.

Adams was a "talker" with a broad and eloquent vocabulary. He spoke clearly and powerfully, with emotion. Regarding his work at the Continental Congress, Jefferson told Daniel Webster, that Adams

"was our Colossus on the floor…with a power, both of thought and of expression which moved us from our seats.".[16]

Another delegate described Adams as,

"the Atlas…He it was who sustained the debate, and by the force of his reasoning demonstrated not only the justice, but the expediency of the measured."[17]

It was Adams who led the debate in favor of the Declaration of Independence and not Jefferson.

Adams' Character Gem No. 10

WORK HARD, COMPETE, AMERICA IS A MERITOCRACY.

Adams criticized both extremes, the idle rich for their snobbery, and anyone who was lazy and wouldn't work. People should be judged on "merit" and society ought to promote upward mobility based on merit. Education was the first step.

Adams' Character Gem No. 11
BE FRUGAL AND NOT EXTRAVAGANT.

Adams had little interest in luxury goods or collecting art, and he was a "plain dresser." He writes,

"Let us have ambition enough to keep our simplicity, our frugality, and our integrity, and transmit these virtues to our children."[18]

Adams' Character Gem No. 12
SUPPORT ORGANIZED RELIGION.

Adams attended church on a regular basis and believed the clergy and organized religion were important to society. He didn't necessarily believe in the miracles described in the Bible.

Adams' Character Gem No. 13
IMPORTANCE OF EDUCATION FOR AN INDIVIDUAL AND FOR SOCIETY-AT-LARGE.

Adams was at the forefront of demanding government support of education for everyone. The Massachusetts Constitution he wrote uniquely endorsed public education. Adams did not come from a wealthy family and he knew his career success was the result of a good education. Moreover, Adams fervently felt that better educational opportunities would lead to a better American culture and to better government.

Adams' Character Gem No. 14
SHAME ON THOSE WITH LOOSE MORALS.

Both John and Abigail were disgusted by the rise in loose morals.

Adams' Character Gem No. 15
BE AGAINST WAR.

"What horrid creatures we men are, that we cannot be virtuous without murdering one another?"[19]

Adams spent much of his term as president keeping the U.S. out of war with France.

Adams' Character Gem No. 16
THERE MUST BE LIMITS ON ANYONE'S POWER AND AUTHORITY.

Adams believed in a stringent set of checks and balances for any institution, company or organization. He preached,

"…that Power was never to be trusted without a Check."[20]

Adams' Character Gem No. 17
DISLIKE POLITICIANS WHO ARE ONLY POLITICIANS.

Adams worried about the honesty of politicians who needed to be re-elected because they had no other skills. Writing to his son about politicians:

"Integrity should be preserved in all events... In order to do this, he must make it a rule to never become dependent on public employments for subsistence. Let him have a trade, a profession, a farm, a shop, something where he can honestly live, and then he may engage in public affairs, if invited, upon independent principles."[21]

Adams' Character Gem No. 18
CULTIVATE AND ENJOY HOBBIES.

Adams enjoyed books, long walks, his pipe and a rural life style.

Jefferson, 1801, painting by Rembrandt Peale

CHAPTER FOUR

PERSONAL CHARACTER VALUES OF PRESIDENT AND CHARACTER PROFESSOR THOMAS JEFFERSON
(1743-1826)
(3rd U.S. President 1801-1809)

IDEALISM CLASHES with REALITY; A BRILLIANT MAN with a COMPLICATED LIFE

> "We hold these truths to be self-evident, that all men are created equal…"
> —THOMAS JEFFERSON,
> Declaration of Independence

"All honor to Jefferson,", said Lincoln, *"to the man who, in the concrete pressure of a struggle for national independence by a single people, had the coolness, forecast, and capacity to introduce into a merely revolutionary document, an abstract truth, applicable to all men and all times, and so to embalm it there, that today, and in all coming days, it shall be a rebuke and a stumbling block to the very harbingers of reappearing tyranny and oppression."*[1]

Jefferson, Adams and Franklin editing the Declaration of Independence

Character Professor Thomas Jefferson

Thomas Jefferson, author of the Declaration of Independence, was well educated and one of the most knowledgeable persons of his era on numerous subjects. He was an idealist and he eloquently set forth the aspirations behind the founding of our nation.

The opposite of his political rival John Adams, Jefferson was friendly, charming and always polite. He loved calmness and order and avoided at all cost confrontations and disputes. Yet during his life he was not always liked by numerous colleagues including George Washington and Alexander Hamilton. Jefferson was ambitious and a fervent partisan politician. Martha Washington felt bitterly toward Jefferson and said the two saddest days of her life were when her husband died and when Jefferson visited her at Mount Vernon, *"the most painful occurrence of her life."*[2] Adams and Jefferson clashed over their political differences and didn't speak or correspond for eleven years. Eventually they did reconcile and regularly exchanged letters over the last fourteen years of their lives.

In part because of financial pressures Jefferson never freed his slaves (Washington freed his slaves in his will) and he carried on a long term relationship with one of his young female slaves.

FAMILY BACKGROUND *and* INFLUENCES *on* JEFFERSON'S CHARACTER

Born in 1743 of English ancestry, Thomas Jefferson was the third child of ten children of Peter and Jane Randolph Jefferson. Father Peter was a wealthy tobacco farmer, surveyor and local judge. Mother Jane was from a wealthy aristocratic

Virginia family. Peter died when Tom was only fourteen. When Tom turned twenty-one he inherited from his father five thousand acres.

Tom was well educated, including by private tutors from age five. He was raised to be a proper aristocratic Virginia plantation owner and gentleman. He was expected to play a public service role in some capacity. He graduated from the College of William and Mary and then studied law, passing the Bar in 1772.

The happiest period of his life was his ten year marriage to Martha ("Patty") Wayles Skelton (1748-1782). Tom and his wife shared the love of music, he playing the violin and she playing the harpsicord. Tom was devastated by her death at age thirty-three. On her deathbed she asked Jefferson, still a young man, to not remarry which he never did.

When not in public service Tom was happily in residence at his beloved plantation Monticello.

CHARACTER PROFESSOR JEFFERSON'S RED WHITE and BLUE CHARACTER GEMS

Jefferson's Character Gem No. 1

BE INTELLECTUALLY CURIOUS AND CHERISH IDEAS AND IDEALS.

Jefferson during his entire life had an unquenchable thirst for knowledge. He simply loved learning. He loved abstract ideas and theories. He wrote about ideals, about how things ought to be. He was also fascinated with architecture, natural science, art, music, food, wine, gardening, and scientific gadgets. He was a Renaissance Man and may have been knowledgeable about more diverse objects than any American of his era, except possibly Ben Franklin.

"Nature intended for me the tranquil pursuits of science, by rendering them my supreme delight."[3]

Jefferson's Character Gem No. 2

AVOID ARGUMENTS, CONFRONTATIONS AND DISORDER.

Jefferson was quiet, somewhat meek and shy, and abhorred disputes or in-person confrontations. He was polite, charming, soft spoken and a good listener. He never argued during a conversation, but chose courtesy over candor. Jefferson:

"…I must not omit the important one of never entering into dispute or argument with another. I never yet saw an instance of one of two disputants convincing the other by argument."[4]

Joseph Ellis in *American Sphinx* points out that he hated the debates in Congress and could not tolerate the bickerings on committees.

"As far as we know, he never rose to deliver a single speech in the Continental Congress…John Adams recalled…during the whole Time I sat with him in Congress, I never heard him utter three sentences together."[5]

When under stress, Jefferson would escape to Monticello, his serene utopia.

Jefferson's Character Gem No. 3
ENJOY AND PROTECT INDIVIDUAL FREEDOM OF RELIGION AND FREEDOM FROM UNDUE GOVERNMENTAL INTERFERENCE.

The basic foundation of Jefferson's ideals is that for people to be happy and live a harmonious life, people need to be free from undue government interference and enjoy freedom of religion.

Jefferson's Character Gem No. 4
ENJOY A BUCOLIC AGRARIAN LIFESTYLE.

Jefferson favored the serenity of a rural life. He viewed,

"great cities as pestilential to the morals, the health and the liberties of man."[6]

"farmers, whose interests are entirely agricultural…are the true representatives of the great American interest, and are alone to be relied on for expressing the proper American sentiments."[7]

Jefferson's Character Gem No. 5
BE OPEN TO CHANGE, FROM ONE GENERATION TO THE NEXT.

Jefferson was completely open to new ideas, new discoveries and events that brought change. He understood that people and institutions had to adapt to changing conditions in order to keep pace. He felt,

"earth belongs in usufruct [right to enjoy] to the living: that the dead have neither powers nor rights over it."[8]

Jefferson's Character Gem No. 6
AVOID UNNECESSARY POMP AND CEREMONY.

Jefferson dressed casually and greeted people in a casual manner, even in the White House when greeting foreign dignitaries.

Jefferson's Character Gem No. 7
APPRECIATE AND LOVE YOUR HOME.

Jefferson was passionate about his plantation, Monticello, which he constantly was remodeling and refurbishing. His home was his heaven where he found peace and could avoid confrontations and disorder.

Jefferson's Character Gem No. 8

TAKE PLEASURE IN BEING A SKILLFUL AND PERHAPS INSPIRATIONAL WRITER.

Jefferson compensated for his dislike of public debate and being a poor verbal communicator by becoming a master with words. His writings were elegant but with straightforward common sense. They were idealistic and inspirational and were the basis of the American dream of freedom and equal opportunity for all. He already had a favorable reputation for his writing skills when he arrived at the Continental Congress. John Adams wrote,

"[He had] a reputation for literature, science, and a happy talent at composition…" [9]

Jefferson's Character Gem No. 9

BE A LOVER OF BOOKS.

Jefferson owned the country's largest private library, which he sold to the U.S. government and became the basis for the Library of Congress. However, he felt novels were "trash" and "a great obstacle to education."

Jefferson's Character Gem No. 10

EDUCATION IS THE CORNERSTONE OF PERSONAL HAPPINESS AND THE CORNERSTONE OF A HARMONIOUS SOCIETY.

Jefferson saw education as a panacea that solved most of society's ills. He felt his founding of the University of Virginia was one of his most important and rewarding accomplishments. Jon Meacham, in *Thomas Jefferson, The Art of Power*, writes *"The three achievements he ordered carved on his tombstone – as author of the American Declaration of Independence and of the Virginia Statute for Religious Liberty, and as founder of the University of Virginia…"*[10]

Jefferson's Character Gem No. 11

IT'S OKAY TO HAVE LOW REGARD FOR LAWYERS.

Although himself a lawyer, he found them to be irritating, always quibbling and full of chicaneries.

Jefferson's Character Gem No. 12

CULTIVATE AND ENJOY HOBBIES.

Jefferson was truly a Renaissance Man and enjoyed art, music (played the violin), gourmet food, natural science, horticulture, scientific tinkering and inventing, books, astronomy, philosophy and a rural lifestyle.

Lincoln with son Tad, 1864

CHAPTER FIVE

PERSONAL CHARACTER VALUES OF PRESIDENT AND CHARACTER PROFESSOR ABRAHAM LINCOLN
(1809-1865)
(16th U.S. President 1861-1865)

A KIND, SENSITIVE, COMPASSIONATE and COMPLEX MAN who MANY BELIEVE was AMERICA'S GREATEST PRESIDENT

> "[Lincoln's bodyguard] Crook had witnessed Lincoln's 'agony when the thunder of the cannon told him that men were being cut down like grass'. He had seen the anguish on the President's face when he came within 'sight of the poor, torn bodies of the dead and dying on the field of Petersburg'…Little wonder that he was overwhelmed at times by a profound sadness that even his own resilient temperament could not dispel."[1]
>
> —DORIS KEARNS GOODWIN
> Team of Rivals, 2005

Lincoln at Antietam, Maryland, 1862

Abraham Lincoln continues, with Franklin, Washington, Adams and Jefferson, the pattern of dissimilar backgrounds and personalities, but all of whom became high achievers and found success. Many historians name Abraham Lincoln as America's greatest president. There is no question but that he was a great person.

For Lincoln, achieving success came only as the result of struggles at every stage of his life. Lincoln's life story is one of poverty, sadness and despair. He found relief being with his family, in his humor and perhaps in his accomplishments. He had few close friends.

Lincoln's despair caused him to look inwardly to learn his strengths and weaknesses and to learn to control his emotions. The result was a man who became comfortable with himself, who was humble and who had empathy and compassion for others.

FAMILY BACKGROUND AND INFLUENCES *on* LINCOLN'S CHARACTER

Lincoln was born in a one room cabin on a small farm in Kentucky in 1809. His parents, Thomas (of English ancestry) and Nancy, were basically illiterate (as was Lincoln's stepmother). The family moved several times from small farm to small farm, from Kentucky to Indiana and then to Illinois. Lincoln's mother died when Lincoln was nine and his father went off to find a new wife when Lincoln was ten, leaving Lincoln and his sister alone for a period of time to fend for themselves. Lincoln's new stepmother was said to be warm and loving toward Lincoln. Her first impression of Lincoln: wild – rugged and dirty. Lincoln had little respect for his father and left home at age twenty-one and moved by himself to New Salem, Illinois.

As a youth in Kentucky and Indiana, Lincoln taught himself to read and write by borrowing books from neighbors. He enthusiastically read every day, especially the Bible, poetry and Shakespeare. He also became a storyteller, blending wit and humor.

In 1860, the *Chicago Tribune* wanted to write Lincoln's biography for the presidential campaign. Lincoln replied,

"The short and simple annals of the poor. That's my life, and that's all you or anyone else can make of it."[2]

In New Salem, Illinois, Lincoln taught himself law. In Springfield, he met Ann Rutledge and fell deeply in love. She died at age twenty-two in 1835 and Lincoln became seriously depressed.

In 1837, Lincoln moved at age twenty-eight to Springfield, Illinois, to commence a law practice. There he met and married Mary Todd (1818-1882). Mary Todd Lincoln was raised in a wealthy family in Lexington, Kentucky. She was said to be vivacious, intelligent and the "belle of the town." She and Lincoln shared a love of poetry and politics, and they were truly devoted to one another. However, Mary was temperamental and mercurial and their marriage was tumultuous. The Lincolns had four children, with Eddie dying at age three, William dying in the White House at age eleven, Tad dying at age eighteen subsequent to the death of Lincoln, with only Robert living to adulthood (1843-1926).

CHARACTER PROFESSOR LINCOLN'S RED WHITE *and* BLUE CHARACTER GEMS

Lincoln's Character Gem No. 1
YOU CAN FIND INNER STRENGTH TO OVERCOME HARDSHIPS AND BOUTS OF DESPAIR.

Lincoln gained inner emotional strength from having suffered and lived through personal hardships. He suffered periods of gloom and despair, which he learned to understand and control. This control of his mood swings served him well and kept him on an even-keel during the low periods of the Civil War, when the North suffered battlefield defeats and thousands of Americans were killed.

When as a young man, having suffered from bouts of depression (and perhaps even being suicidal), Lincoln survived and was able to counsel others. In a letter to a West Point student, he encouraged the boy:

"I am older than you, have felt badly myself, and know, what I tell you is true. Adhere to your purpose and you will soon feel as well as you ever did. On the contrary, if you falter, and give up, you will lose the power of keeping any resolution, and will regret it all your life."[3]

The boy stayed at West Point, graduating in 1866.

Lincoln's Character Gem No. 2

KNOW YOURSELF! BE INTROSPECTIVE AND SELF-AWARE OF YOUR STRENGTHS AND WEAKNESSES.

Perhaps because of personal difficulties in early life, Lincoln was somewhat of a loner and introspective. Throughout his life, he would withdraw and be deep in thought. He was realistic about himself and his strengths and weaknesses. This was an essential strength of Lincoln – knowing who he was. Introspective self-awareness gave him inner peace.

Lincoln's Character Gem No. 3

TO SUCCEED YOU MUST RESOLVE TO SUCCEED, BE SELF-RELIANT AND A SELF-STARTER.

Lincoln clearly proved that America is the land of opportunity. He was born into poverty, had only one year of schooling and suffered numerous hardships. Yet Lincoln had confidence, relied on himself and through hard work, persistence and unquenchable ambition, found success. Giving advice to a youth, Lincoln wrote,

"Always bear in mind that your own resolution to succeed is more important than any other one thing."[4]

Lincoln's Character Gem No. 4
HUMILITY. IT WILL MAKE YOU A BETTER PERSON, COLLEAGUE, AND LEADER.

Understanding his strengths and weaknesses led Lincoln to be humble, to gladly surround himself in his cabinet with better educated colleagues (including past political rivals), to admit mistakes, to admit what he didn't know, to be a good listener, and to continue to learn, evolve and adapt throughout his life.

Commenting on Lincoln's humility and lack of ego, a fellow Illinois lawyer wrote,

"It required no effort on his part to admit another man's superiority."[5]

Lincoln also was willing to share credit for success, and wrote,

"Path to success and ambition is broad enough for two."[6]

Some historians believe Lincoln was the least egotistical person who became president.

Lincoln's Character Gem No. 5
HAVE EMPATHY AND COMPASSION FOR OTHERS.

Lincoln was perhaps our most human and humane president. Doris Kearns Goodwin in Team of Rivals writes,

"Lincoln's abhorrence of hurting another was born of more than simple compassion. He possessed extraordinary empathy – the gift or curse of putting himself in the place of another, to experience what they were feeling, to understand their motives and desires."[7]

Most famously, of course, his compassion was shown in his benevolent policy of no punishment of the Confederate soldiers at the end of the Civil War, but rather allowing them to return to their homes, taking their horses and side-arms with them.

From his most famous speech, the Second Inaugural, he spoke:

"With malice toward none; with charity for all; with firmness in the right, as God gives us to see the right, let us strive on to finish the work we are in; to bind up the nation's wounds; to care for him who shall have borne the battle, and for his widow, and his orphan – to do all which may achieve and cherish a just, and a lasting peace, among ourselves, and with all nations."[8]

Lincoln's Character Gem No. 6

HUMOR IS HEALTHY AND IMPORTANT, ESPECIALLY AT TIMES OF STRESS.

Lincoln was a great storyteller and he used humor as his relaxation. His close friend, Joshua Speed, remarked,

"His storytelling…was necessary to his very existence… he sought relaxation in anecdotes."[9]

He used humor to overcome his own gloomy feelings, but also importantly to relieve stress and anxiety within his cabinet during the war. He encouraged a relaxed atmosphere.

Lincoln's Treasury Secretary Hugh McCullough:

"...story-telling was to him a safety-valve and that he indulged in it, not only for the pleasure it afforded him, but for a temporary relief from oppressing cares."[10]

Lincoln's Character Gem No. 7

BE LIKE HONEST ABE! HONESTY AND TRUTH MUST BE THE CORNERSTONE OF YOUR CHARACTER.

Lincoln, as a trial lawyer in the 1850's, found much success because of his emphasis on hard cold facts. He was a seeker of truth. He was both morally honest and intellectually honest. He was Honest Abe, and won lawsuits without legal tricks or shenanigans, but because the judges knew he spoke the truth.

Friend Jesse W. Fell wrote:

"If there were any traits of character that stood out in bold relief, in the person of Mr. Lincoln, it was that of Truth, and Candor. He was utterly incapable of insincerity...In the grand review of his peculiar characteristics, nothing creates such an impressive effect as his love of the truth."[11]

Law partner William H. Herndon on Abe:

"…he was the very essence and substance of truth; and was of unbounded veracity, had unlimited integrity, always telling the truth and always doing the honest thing at all times and under all circumstances."[12]

David Herbert Donald, in Lincoln, writes:

"He became known as 'Honest Abe' – or, often 'Honest Old Abe' – the lawyer who was never known to lie. He held himself to the highest standards of truthfulness."[13]

Lincoln's Character Gem No. 8
DON'T BE AFRAID TO SPEAK FROM THE HEART.

Without formal schooling, Lincoln educated himself through books he borrowed from neighbors. He became a masterful speech writer and eloquent orator. His speeches usually included wit and humorous storytelling. He would turn life experiences into meaningful anecdotes. Reporter Horme wrote,

"His [Lincoln] speaking went to the heart because it came from the heart. I have heard celebrated orators who could start thunders of applause without changing any man's opinion. Mr. Lincoln's eloquence was of a higher type, which produced conviction in others because of the conviction of the speaker himself."[14]

He was able to blend humor, wit and logic, and concisely express his message. The Gettysburg Address was only two hundred and seventy-two words.

Lincoln's Character Gem No. 9
TURN THE OTHER CHEEK AND FORGIVE.

Throughout his life when Lincoln suffered insubordination by others or hurtful criticism from a colleague, Lincoln turned the other cheek, forgave and was not vindictive as most people (including most presidents) might be. On one such occasion Lincoln's aide John Nicolay wrote,

"Probably no other man than Lincoln would have had, in this age of the world, the degree of magnanimity to thus forgive and exalt a rival who had so deeply and so unjustifiably intrigued against him. It is however only another most marked illustration of the greatness of this President."[15]

At times when frustrated with a colleague, he would get over his anger by writing a letter to the colleague thereby venting his anger, but wouldn't send it.

Lincoln's Character Gem No. 10
BE CAUTIOUS, BUT WITH AN EFFECTIVE SENSE OF TIMING.

Part of Lincoln's genius as a leader was his excellent sense of timing. He was cautious by nature and didn't want to get too far out in front of his colleagues on the issues. He knew timing was critical, when to act and when to wait. He wrote,

"A man watches his pear tree day after day, impatient for the ripening of the fruit. Let him attempt to force the process, and he may spoil both fruit and tree. But let him patiently wait, and the ripe pear at length falls into his lap!"[16]

Lincoln's Character Gem No. 11
BE PRACTICAL BUT DON'T DESERT YOUR PRINCIPLES.

In war time, Lincoln had to take a pragmatic approach to most problems. Lincoln knew that to win the war he had to maintain support of numerous diverse factions within the northern states. However, this never caused him to desert his base principles and convictions. His rock solid principles gave him vision and direction. David Herbert Donald, in Lincoln wrote,

"But on one point he was immovable: the extension of slavery into the national territories…Let there be no compromise… Stand firm…"[17]

Mary Lincoln observed,

"He was a terribly firm man when he set his foot down."[18]

Lincoln's Character Gem No. 12
THE END GOAL IS ESTEEM FROM YOUR PEERS, NOT WEALTH ACCUMULATION OR CELEBRITY.

The driving ambition that kept Lincoln moving forward through his personal hardships and carried him to greatness was his need for the esteem of his peers. It was not for wealth or to be a celebrity. At age twenty-three, Lincoln wrote,

"I can say for one that I have no other [ambition] so great as that of being truly esteemed of my fellow men, by rendering myself worthy of their esteem."[19]

Character Professor Abraham Lincoln

Lincoln's Character Gem No. 13
CULTIVATE AND ENJOY HOBBIES.

Lincoln enjoyed humor and storytelling, cats, theater and chess; he did not drink alcohol or smoke.

Grant, 1880, painting by Thomas LeClear

CHAPTER SIX

PERSONAL CHARACTER VALUES OF PRESIDENT AND CHARACTER PROFESSOR ULYSSES S. GRANT
(1822 – 1885)
(18th U.S. PRESIDENT, 1869-1877)

WAR HERO *and as* PRESIDENT PROTECTOR *of the* RIGHTS *of* 4,000,000 FREED SLAVES

"What a man he is! What a history! What an illustration - his life - of the capacities of that American individuality common to us all. Cynical critics are wondering 'what the people see in Grant' to make such a hubbub about. They aver…that he has hardly the average of our day's literary and scholastic culture, and absolutely no pronounc'd genius or conventional eminence of any sort. Correct: but he proves how an average western farmer, mechanic, boatman, carried by tides of circumstances, perhaps caprices, into a position of incredible military or civil responsibilities…may steer his way fitly and steadily through them all, carrying the country and himself with credit year after year – command over a million armed men – fight more than fifty pitch'd battles – rule for eight years a land larger than all the kingdoms of Europe combined."[1]

—WALT WHITMAN

Grant at Cold Harbor Virginia, 1864

There is considerable surprising information when learning about Ulysses S. Grant, including that his real name is Hiram Ulysses Grant. A successful military leader in a horrific bloody war, yet also a loving family man, who was quiet, low-key, humble and compassionate. Mark Twain called him a "lovable great child." He was honest, loyal to a fault and a humanitarian who sent troops to battle the Klu Klux Klan. He liked to sketch and paint, similar to another president who was also a military hero, Dwight Eisenhower.

FAMILY BACKGROUND *and* INFLUENCES *on* GRANT'S CHARACTER

Hiram Ulysses was born in Ohio in 1822, the first of six children of Jesse Grant (1794-1873) and Hannah Simpson Grant (1798-1883). Jesse, of English ancestry, was a farmer and moderately successful owner of a leather tanning business. He is said to have been somewhat arrogant and a bit too boisterous and outgoing. Not much is known of Hannah, of Scottish Protestant ancestry, other than she was the opposite of Jesse, quiet, serious and devoting religious (Methodist). Grant as an adult was not close to either parent and for some unknown reason his mother never visited him at the White House.

Grant disliked farming and to a greater extent disliked the tanning business, especially the blood and the odors. He became a skilled horseman at a young age and gained a reputation in the community for breaking and training young colts. He was only an average student but through some luck and political friends of his father he was accepted at West Point. He was not a hard worker or very ambitious prior to or at West

Point but managed to graduate in the middle of his class.

Grant's first posting after graduation was outside St. Louis where in 1844 he met his wife, Julia Boggs (1826-1902), the daughter of a plantation owner. She was intelligent, relatively well-educated and social, having grown up in the St. Louis upper class "society". She played the piano and her interests included music, literature and horses.

Grant served in several military posts, finally resigning from the military in 1854 while stationed in the Pacific Northwest, perhaps the result of loneliness and drunkenness.

Grant returned to the St. Louis area and then to Galena, Illinois, where he and Julia suffered through seven years of business failures. Jean Edward Smith in his biography *Grant* tells us:,

"On December 23, 1857 he pawned his gold pocket watch – his last valuable possession – so his family might have money to celebrate Christmas. [Later] Grant was reduced to once more to peddling firewood on St. Louis street corners."[2]

In 1861 upon the breakout of the Civil War, Grant rejoined the Army and organized a group of Galena volunteers to be known as the 21st Illinois Regiment. The Civil War gave Grant a new beginning, an opportunity to go from failure to success. Military strategy and leading men into battle turned out to be his calling.

Grant and his wife Julia shared an unconditional love for one another. She continued to give him love and emotional support through both the good times and the bad times. They had a happy family life and raised four children.

Grant battled alcoholism throughout his life, which he essentially overcame while president. Chernow in *Grant* concludes,

"...Grant managed to attain mastery over alcohol in the long haul, a feat as impressive as any of his wartime victories."[3]

CHARACTER PROFESSOR GRANT'S RED WHITE *and* BLUE CHARACTER GEMS

Grant's Character Gem No. 1
FIND SUCCESS BY FOLLOWING YOUR PASSION.

Grant is the quintessential example of a person who found his passion late in life and was able to combine his passion and career. War transformed a failure of a man into a hero. He found his passion and he blossomed. Ron Chernow in his book *Grant* states,

"Suddenly Grant was fired by a mission, a clear sense of purpose, something that had been lacking in the 1850's. He was now wide awake, his pulse quickened by an overriding sense of duty."[4]

The matching of his passion and a career dramatically changed his life for the better.

Grant's Character Gem No. 2
BE A DOER! DON'T PROCRASTINATE OR LOOK FOR EXCUSES.

Simply said, Grant got things done. He didn't procrastinate and didn't look for excuses. He started a project, was persistent, and didn't stop until the work was done. Lincoln replaced General after General because of their inactivity, then he found Grant. As Lincoln said,

"Things move wherever he is."[5]

and Lincoln said:

"The great thing about Grant is his perfect coolness and persistency of purpose…and he has the grit of a bulldog. Once let him get his teeth in, and nothing can shake him off."[6]

Grant's Character Gem No. 3
BE A FAMILY PERSON!

Grant loved and enjoyed his family. Grant and his wife, Julia, shared mutual unconditional love. Grant was extremely lonely without her. They endured through failures and forced separations but then enjoyed success. Grant during the courtship, wrote,

"You can have but little idea of the influence you have over me Julia, even while so far away. If I feel tempted to do anything that I think is not right I am shure to think, 'Well now if Julia saw me would I do so' and thus it is absent or present I am more or less governed by what I think is your will."[7]

Grant was a responsible, kind and loving father to his four children. He was not a strict disciplinarian and one of Grant's staff officers recalled,

"The children often romped with him and he joined in their frolics as if they were all playmates together. The younger ones would hang around his neck while he was writing, make a terrible mess of the papers, and turn everything in his tent into a toy."[8]

Chernow writes:

"Grant had two congenial weaknesses, children and horses, and was gentle with both. 'I have never known a man who had such nice ways about him in that respect as my father' said Fred [his son]."[9]

Grant's Character Gem No. 4

BE LIKE GRANT. IF NECESSARY, YOU TOO CAN OVERCOME FAILURE AND HUMILIATION.

On numerous occasions, Grant was a failure and felt humiliated. From this Grant developed a quiet inner strength and he never quit but persevered.

Jean Edward Smith, in the Preface to his biography Grant summarizes,

"The common thread is strength of character – an indomitable will that never flagged in the face of adversity…There was something mysterious about him – a deep, primal force that sustained him through defeat and humiliation."[10]

Grant's Character Gem No. 5

QUIET DIGNITY! BE HUMBLE, BE LOW KEY, BE A "REGULAR GUY" WITHOUT PRETENSIONS.

"Grant did not look like a President any more than he looked like a general."[11]

Humility was one of the cornerstones of Grant's character. He didn't let success go to his head and he never put on airs or acted in a superior manner. He was popular with the troops because he was a regular guy without pretensions. He felt good deeds spoke for themselves. People who met him for the first time, even after his presidency, were surprised at his quiet low key disposition and his understated dress and manners.

James L. Crane, Chaplain, 21st Illinois wrote:

"He usually wore a plain blue blouse coat, and an ordinary black felt hat, and never had about him a single mark to distinguish his rank."[12]

Chernow wrote,

"The plain unadorned Grant had nothing stylish about him, leading sophisticated people to underrate his talents. He was a nondescript face in the crowd, the common man from the heartland raised to a higher power, who proved a simple Westerner could lead a mighty army to victory and occupy the Presidential chair with distinction."[13]

Grant's Character Gem No. 6

WHEN OTHERS SUFFER HARDSHIP, SHOW RESPECT AND COMPASSION.

Grant knew failure and hardship intimately. In the latter half of the 1850's, while married and trying to support a growing family, he was poor, out of a job and lacked direction. When success came he never forgot this suffering and was merciful and compassionate in victory. There was no celebration or exaltation at Appomattox, and he offered magnanimous and compassionate peace terms to Robert E. Lee and his troops. He even sent food to the Confederate troops, and allowed them to keep their horses and mules for plowing.

Grant's Character Gem No. 7
BE LOYAL TO FAMILY, FRIENDS AND COLLEAGUES.

Grant was extremely loyal to others, overlooking at times mistakes and giving most people second or third chances. Unfortunately, while president this became problematic when members of his administration entered into dishonest activities.

Grant's Character Gem No. 8
BE GENTLE AND KIND TO OTHERS.

Contrary to what one imagines is the personality of a great military leader, Grant was polite, gentle and kind. Mark Twain called him a lovable great child,

> "His exceeding gentleness, kindness, forbearance, lovingness, charity…he was the most lovable great child in the world."[14]

Grant's Character Gem No. 9
KEEP YOUR COOL! REMAIN CALM.

Grant was quiet, even tempered and never argumentative. Even when at war, including when dodging bullets, he was unflappable and able to stay calm.

Grant's Character Gem No. 10
NO NEED TO SWEAR.

Grant never swore. He was raised in this manner in a Methodist household by his mother. Grant wrote,

"It has been a principle of mine never to swear at any time in my life."[15]

"When a boy I seemed to have an aversion to it, and when I became a man, I saw the folly of it…swearing helps rouse a man's anger; and when a man flies into a passion, his adversary who keeps his cool, always gets the better of him. [Swearing] is a great waste of time."[16]

Grant's Character Gem No. 11
APPRECIATE THE VALUE OF A QUALITY ASSISTANT.

Grant knew he needed the assistance of others at each stage of his career. He especially appreciated the help of a day-to-day close personal assistant.

Grant's Character Gem No. 12
RESPECT AND ASSIST AMERICA'S MINORITY GROUPS.

Grant was a humanitarian. He struggled against great odds to protect and provide justice and civil rights for newly freed African Americans and for Native Americans. Frederick Douglass is quoted as saying that Grant was, "the vigilant, firm, impartial, and wise protector of my race."[17]

Historian Sean Wilentz states:

"The evidence clearly shows that [Grant] created the most auspicious record on racial equality and civil rights of any President from Lincoln to Lyndon B. Johnson."[18]

Grant's Character Gem No. 13
DO NOT AGGRANDIZE OR ROMANTICIZE WAR.

The epitaph on Grant's tomb reads *"Let us have peace,"*[19] which memorializes Grant's own words upon acceptance of the presidential nomination. He remarked,

"I never went into a battle willingly or with enthusiasm…It is at all times a sad and cruel business. I hate war with all my heart…"[20]

However, he was a mastermind at war strategy and also able to improvise in the field. He was a "muddy boots general," on numerous times ducking bullets, and not a "desk general."

Grant's Character Gem No. 14
CULTIVATE AND ENJOY HOBBIES.

Grant enjoyed horses, sketching and painting (watercolors), chess, playing cards, cigars (died of throat cancer).

Roosevelt when in the Amazon after his presidency, 1910

CHAPTER SEVEN

PERSONAL CHARACTER VALUES OF PRESIDENT AND CHARACTER PROFESSOR THEODORE ROOSEVELT
(1858 – 1919)
(26th U.S. President, 1901-1909)

OUTDOORSMAN, LOVER *of* **NATURE** *and of* **STRENUOUS ACTIVITY, WHO** *as* **PRESIDENT FOUGHT AGAINST EXCESSIVE GREED** *and* **POLITICAL CORRUPTION** *and* **PROTECTED AMERICA'S NATURAL RESOURCES**

"It is not the critic who counts, not the man who points out how the strong man stumbles, or where the doer of deeds could have done better. The credit belongs to the man who is actually in the arena, whose face is marred by dust and sweat and blood; who strives valiantly; who errs, and comes short again and again, because there is not effort without error and shortcoming; but who does actually strive to do the deeds; who knows the great enthusiasms, the great devotions; who spends himself in a worthy cause."[1]

—THEODORE ROOSEVELT

TR with silver Bowie knife from Tiffany's when in the Badlands after death of wife, 1885

Colonel Roosevelt of the Rough Riders, 1898

Theodore Roosevelt
Col 1st U S V cavalry

Roosevelt with wife Edith and their six children, 1903

Roosevelt with John Muir

Character Professor Theodore Roosevelt

"Now look, that damned cowboy is President of the United States."[2]

—MARK HANNA,
leader of Roosevelt's own political party

"You only have to live with me, while I have to live with you."[3]

—WIFE EDITH ROOSEVELT,
who in a friendly way reminded TR of this on a regular basis

"He had seen two tremendous works of nature in America — the Niagara Falls and Mr. Roosevelt." [4]

—A BRITISH VISCOUNT

'*My father always wanted to be the corpse at every funeral, the bride at every wedding, and the baby at every christening.*"[5]

—DAUGHTER ALICE

Talent, energy, persistence and ego are a few of the words which describe Theodore Roosevelt. He lived every day to its utmost, had a "bully good time" and always carried a "Big Stick." He had as large an impact on the history of America as any other president. He became president at a transformational time when the Industrial Revolution had created huge economic disparities between Americans. Powerful monopolies crushed competition and crushed lives. TR tried to even the competition between producer and consumer, between big business and small business, and between robber barons and America's natural resources.

America needed someone of talent, energy, persistence and ego, and they found one in Theodore Roosevelt.

FAMILY BACKGROUND *and* INFLUENCES *on* TR'S CHARACTER

Theodore Roosevelt (Don't call me Teddy!) was born into wealth in New York City in 1858 to parents Theodore and Martha ("Millie") Bulloch Roosevelt. Father Theodore, principally of Dutch ancestry, was independently wealthy and noted for his significant philanthropy. He was one of the initial founders of the New York Children's Orthopedic Hospital, the New York City Children's Aid Society, the Metropolitan Museum of Art and the American Museum of Natural History. To TR, his father was "the best man I ever knew." Mother Millie was a beautiful Georgia southern belle whose brothers fought for the Confederacy. Cleanliness was one of Millie's passions and she usually dressed in white.

TR was the second of four children. He was especially

close his entire life to his older sister Anna, known as Bamie, including consulting her during his presidency. First Lady Eleanor Roosevelt, wife of President Franklin Roosevelt, was the daughter of TR's younger brother Elliott.

TR was a sickly, frail and timid youth in part because of horrific asthma attacks. He turned to books, especially about nature. He studied bugs, birds, flowers, reptiles and other animals of all types and even became an amateur taxidermist. A milestone in his young life was when at age eleven, he received thick spectacles to assist his nearsightedness and received a shotgun. Equally important, TR followed his father's advice that he begin a physical training program to develop his frail body and to build confidence. TR vigorously plunged into a routine that included weights, running, swimming and boxing lessons.

He never ceased loving nature and was constantly sketching and filling up notebooks with information on his specimens, which he housed in his personal Roosevelt Museum of Natural History on the fourth floor of his New York City home.

TR had a peculiar voice and manner of speaking, described by his mother as *"an ungreased squeak."*[6]

Other descriptions:

"He spewed words with a force that often startled people."[7]

[He] "sort of spluttered as he spoke – his thoughts charging on faster than his mouth could handle them."[8]

"His large and extremely white teeth appeared to chop sentences to pieces."[9]

HEAR YE! HEAR YE!

"Words tumbled over one another."[10]

"Ejaculating the words like bullets."[11]

He attended Harvard and graduated Phi Beta Kappa. Most of TR's classmates found him rather eccentric. His room was overflowing with stuffed snakes, lizards and birds and he spoke rapidly and never stopped talking. One professor had to shut him up by saying,

"See here Roosevelt, let me talk, I'm running this class."[12]

In his junior year he met and immediately fell deeply in love and married Alice Hathaway Lee, from a socially prominent family in Chestnut Hill, Massachusetts. TR adored Alice and this was an extremely happy time of TR's life.

Double tragedy struck in 1884 when on the same day both his wife Alice and his mother died in their joint New York City home. His mother died at age forty-eight from typhoid fever and wife Alice from kidney failure at age twenty-two, two days after giving birth to baby Alice.

TR was devastated. He wrote about Alice,

"The light has gone out of my life."[13]

He fled to live alone in the Badlands of the Dakota Territories. He became a cowboy, including in dress and with his pearl handled revolver. He invested in two cattle ranches and at one time had over 5,000 head of cattle. His days were difficult and he spent many lonely hours on horseback. He became an avid hunter of deer, bear, buffalo and antelope.

David McCullough in *Mornings on Horseback* writes,

> "The Badlands were 'dreary and forbidding', they were 'as grim and desolate and forbidding as any spot on earth could be', and he felt he belonged… The words 'loneliness' and 'solitude' appear repeatedly in what he [TR] wrote. He writes again and again of 'great dreary solitude' and 'melancholy pathless plains', 'the deathlike stillness'."[14]

On a visit back to New York he spent time with Edith Carow, who also came from a wealthy socially prominent New York family. TR returned to the Badlands but eventually sold his cattle ranches and married Edith. TR and Edith had a loving, happy marriage and raised a family of six children. Edith was calm, reserved and less gregarious than TR and so was Yin to his Yang.

CHARACTER PROFESSOR TR'S
RED WHITE *and* BLUE CHARACTER GEMS

TR's Character Gem No. 1
LIVE EVERY DAY TO ITS UTMOST WITH THROTTLE WIDE OPEN.

TR loved life. Life was to him a great adventure to be lived to its fullest with throttle wide open. One of his favorite mottos was "Get Action, Do Things.". He once said,

"I like to drink the wine of life with brandy in it."[15]

Henry Adams (of the renowned political Adams family) saw TR as,

"Chewing his way through his future like a buzz saw, always busy and fully engaged, exploiting his chief quality which was the ability to live intensely every thought."[16]

Others described him using such words as whirlwind, perpetual motion, needing excitement, steam train, energetic, vigorous, high spirited, frenetic, tireless, and exuberant.
   A New York assemblyman's view:

"He came in as if he had been ejected by a catapult."[17]

TR's Character Gem No. 2

COMPETE, ENJOY A GOOD FIGHT AND GROW AS A PERSON THROUGH A "STRENUOUS LIFE."

TR thrived and was at his best when competing, struggling, fighting, either physically or mentally. He truly believed that the only way a person grew in character or achieved any meaningful success was through struggle.

TR regularly wrote and preached about the benefits of "The Strenuous Life",

"…the highest form of success comes…to the man who does not shrink from danger, from hardship, or from bitter toil."[18]

Biographer Bazalgette in Theodore Roosevelt said it best:

"To live, for him (TR), has no meaning other than to drive oneself, to act with all one's strength. An existence without stress, without struggle, without growth, has always struck him as mindless."[19]

McCullough, in Mornings on Horseback,

"He was never more pleased with himself than when he had made a "stout fight". The political allies he cared most for were those who were fighters, who were fearless…"[20]

Vice President Thomas Marshall,

"Death had to take him sleeping, for if Roosevelt had been awake, there would have been a fight."[21]

TR's Character Gem No. 3

PARTAKE IN PHYSICAL EXERCISE EVERY DAY.

For TR, leading a "Strenuous Life" includes daily physical exercise, in part as a test of manliness. While president, this included early morning tennis with his self-anointed "Tennis Cabinet," wrestling, boxing (until a blow caused permanent damage to his left eye), jujitsu, skinny dipping in the Potomac, plus horseback galloping, hiking and rock climbing in Rock Creek Park.

TR's Character Gem No. 4

BE CHEERFUL, BE OPTIMISTIC, ENJOY HUMOR AND LAUGHTER AND HAVE A BULLY GOOD TIME.

TR was joyfully optimistic about his personal future and the future of the nation. This optimism was infectious to those he met and to the nation as a whole. Historian Lewis L. Gould described TR's persona as,

"a roman candle of exuberance and fun."[22]

Renowned newspaperman, William Allen White, once described TR as,

"He seemed full of animal spirits, exhaustless at all hours, exuding cheer and confidence."[23]

TR's biographer, Edmund Morris, wrote about a reporter who spent a week with TR who calculated, *"laughed, on average, a hundred times a day – and what was more, laughed heartily. He laughs like an irresponsible schoolboy on a lark, his face flushing ruddy, his eyes nearly closed, his utterance choked with merriment, his speech abandoned for a weird falsetto…"*[24]

A British diplomat described the spirited exuberance of TR the best,

"You must remember that the President is about six (years old)."[25]

TR's Character Gem No. 5

ACTIVITY, ACTIVITY AND MORE ACTIVITY CAN HELP OVERCOME SADNESS AND DESPAIR.

TR turned to constant activity to heal from the deaths of his wife and mother. He fled to the Dakota Badlands and the rigorous life as a cowboy, on some days spending eighteen hours on horseback.

TR hoped that depression wouldn't catch him if he kept moving, and wrote,

"Black care rarely sits behind a rider whose pace is fast enough."[26]

TR's Character Gem No. 6
HAVE COURAGE TO LEAVE YOUR COMFORT ZONE.

TR was fearless and didn't worry about making mistakes. At a young age, as directed by his father, TR gained confidence by putting aside books and animal studies to commence bodybuilding to overcome his frailty.

Goodwin in *The Bully Pulpit* described TR's initial apprehension upon leaving his comfort zone,

"Transforming his body was the only one step in the psychological struggle against what Teedie shamefully considered his 'timid' nature." "There were all kinds of things of which I was afraid at first," he acknowledged, *"but by acting as if I was not afraid I gradually ceased to be afraid."*[27]

As a childhood friend observed,

"by constantly forcing himself to do the difficult or even dangerous thing, he was able to cultivate courage as a matter of habit, in the sense of repeated effort and repeated exercise of will power."[28]

When the Spanish-American War broke out, TR left his then comfort zone as Assistant Secretary of the Navy to charge up San Juan Hill in Cuba with his Rough Riders.

"I had a bully time and a bully fight."[29]

TR's Character Gem No. 7

LEARN ABOUT AND ENJOY NATURE AND THE GREAT OUTDOORS.

TR from a young age was a student and lover of nature. He read about, made sketches of and collected and mounted bug, bird and animal specimens for his personal Roosevelt Museum of Natural History on the fourth floor of his New York City home. His father hired a professional taxidermist to train TR. At age eleven TR received his first shotgun and he became an avid hunter and outdoorsman. He had a special love of birds and was a fervent supporter of numerous nature organizations including the Audubon Society. Some conservationists refer to TR's three day camping trip in 1903 with naturalist John Muir to the giant sequoia trees of the Mariposa Grove, and then the valley floor of Yosemite, as the most important camping trip in America's history.

TR's Character Gem No. 8

ENJOY FAMILY. "THE BEST CROP IS THE CROP OF CHILDREN."

Family meant everything to TR. His father was his best friend and he deeply loved his mother. Growing up, the Roosevelt homes in New York City and Oyster Bay were constantly overflowing with uncles, aunts, cousins, nieces and nephews. Same held true with the homes of TR and Edith, including the White House. To TR…*"the best crop is the crop of children."*[30] Even while president, evening was reserved for reading adventure novels and poetry to his children, plus pillow fights, wrestling, playing "bear" and other games.

TR's Character Gem No. 9

ADOPT THE PERSONAL CHARACTER VALUES OF THE AMERICAN COWBOY.

The personal character values of hard work, honesty, courage and overall righteousness were taught to TR by his father and reinforced by TR's experience living in the Badlands.

To explain TR's value system and why TR had such high praise for both the American Cowboy and his father, McCullough writes:

"...he wrote of the cowboy with an appreciation not to be found in the work of previous writers...he wrote of their courage, their phenomenal physical endurance. He liked their humor, admired the unwritten code that ruled the cow camp. 'Meanness, cowardice, and dishonesty are not tolerated', he observed. 'There is a high regard for truthfulness and keeping one's word, intense contempt for any kind of hypocrisy, and a hearty dislike for a man who shirks his work.' It was, of course, exactly the code he had been raised on."[31]

TR's Character Gem No. 10

ENJOY READING, AND READ IN "TIME USUALLY WASTED."

Being a frail and sickly youth, TR turned to books for his enjoyment, especially on nature and adventure. For TR books were the "greatest of companions" and he became a voracious reader. He wrote,

"It is surprising how much reading a man can do in time usually wasted."[32]

TR's Character Gem No. 11
BE INTELLECTUALLY CURIOUS.

"Everything was of interest to him," marveled the French Ambassador Jean Jules Jusserand, *"people of today, people of yesterday, animals, minerals, stones, stars, the past, the future."*[33]

TR's Character Gem No. 12
BE WILLING TO COMPROMISE, BALANCE, WORK WITH OTHERS.

TR was a great fighter, but knew when to back off and be a "centralist" to get results. He was a bold leader, but for "moderate" reform.

"I thereby learned the invaluable lesson that in the practical activities of life no man can render the highest service unless he can act in combination with his fellows, which means a certain amount of give-and-take between him and them."[34]

TR's Character Gem No. 13
BE TENACIOUS AND PERSISTENT UNTIL YOU REACH YOUR GOAL.

TR never did anything halfway. When he proposed to Alice Lee and she turned him down, he announced, *"She won't have me, but I will have her."*[35] So commenced an epic quest of wooing; he pursued her and *"made everything subordinate to winning her."*[36]

When an assassin lodged a bullet in his chest in Milwaukee during his last presidential campaign, he delivered his speech anyway and then went to the hospital.

"Bleeding heavily, he told the stunned crowd, 'I have just been shot, but it takes more than that to kill a Bull Moose.' Apparently, his text and a case in his vest pocket slowed the bullet."[37]

TR's Character Gem No. 14
CULTIVATE AND ENJOY HOBBIES.

TR enjoyed horseback riding, reading and writing, outdoors and nature, boxing, swimming, hiking, tennis, hunting, and attending church. His love of animals can be shown in the number of White House pets for his six children, which included guinea pigs, a hen ("Baron Spreckle"), lizard ("Bill"), Manchester terrier, macaw ("Eli Yale"), garter snake ("Emily Spinach"), small brown bear ("Jonathan Edwards"), rat ("Jonathon"), badger ("Josiah"), pig ("Mavre"), Saint Bernard ("Rollo"), cats ("Tom Quartz" and "Slippers"), numerous dogs (one favorite being "Pete", a bull terrier), and eight horses (a favorite being "Bleistein"), plus two ponies ("General Grant" and "Algonquin").

William Howard Taft, painting by Anders Leonard Zorn, 1911

CHAPTER EIGHT

PERSONAL CHARACTER VALUES OF PRESIDENT AND CHARACTER PROFESSOR WILLIAM HOWARD TAFT

(1857-1930)

(27th U.S. President 1909-1913)

(Chief Justice of the Supreme Court 1921-1930)

"MR. NICE GUY" WHO WAS PERHAPS TOO WILLING TO PLEASE OTHERS

"He is the best man I have ever known, too honest for the Presidency, possibly, and possibly too good natured or too trusting or too something."[1]

—TAFT'S WHITE HOUSE AIDE ARCHIE BUTT

"...the honest greenhorn at the poker table."[2]

—JOURNALIST CHARLES THOMPSON

300 pound, avid golfer Taft playing golf at Seattle Golf Club, 1909

William Howard Taft had little interest in politics and little interest in being president of the United States. His wife Nellie wanted him to be president, his brother James wanted him to be president, and Theodore Roosevelt wanted him to be president. Taft wanted to be a judge like his father. Taft's ultimate dream was to be Chief Justice of the U.S. Supreme Court, which he ultimately achieved after his presidency. Taft tried to always remain a "nice guy" even after the disappointment of not being reelected in 1912 as the result of his previous best friend Roosevelt forming a splinter political party in 1912. This allowed Democrat Woodrow Wilson in a three party race to be elected with less than a majority of the votes. During the campaign Roosevelt attacked Taft in cutting personal ways, including calling him a "fathead.".

    His career and life had a happy ending. Subsequent to his presidency he was appointed Chief Justice of the Supreme Court and served in this capacity for nine years.

FAMILY BACKGROUND *and* INFLUENCES *on* TAFT'S CHARACTER

William Howard Taft, primarily of English descent, was born in 1857 in Cincinnati, Ohio, the son of Alphonso Taft, a lawyer, judge, U.S. Attorney General and Secretary of War under President Grant, and Ambassador to Austria-Hungary and Russia under President Chester Arthur. His mother Louise, a graduate of Mount Holyoke College was "enormously energetic, aggressively intellectual, and decidedly ambitious." Many historians believe Taft never successfully cut his umbilical cord and always suffered from anxiety and felt pressure to please his ambitious parents.

Taft went to Yale, graduating through hard work second in his class. He returned to Cincinnati to study law at Cincinnati Law School. He married Helen "Nellie" Herron, the daughter of a prominent Cincinnati lawyer. She visited the White House as a youth with her parents, began wishing to become First Lady herself and reportedly vowed to marry only a man "destined to be President of the United States." This seemingly unimportant event, Nellie's visit to the White House, was perhaps the singular best (or worst?) influence on Taft's career.

Taft and wife Nellie had two sons and a daughter, each of which had successful careers of their own. Son Robert was elected to the U.S. Senate in 1938 and served until his death in 1953.

HEAR YE! HEAR YE!

CHARACTER PROFESSOR TAFT'S RED WHITE and BLUE CHARACTER GEMS

Taft's Character Gem No. 1

ACHIEVE HAPPINESS, FRIENDSHIPS AND SUCCESS BY BEING EASYGOING AND A "GOOD GUY".

Taft was said to have the *"sunny disposition of an innocent child."*[3] He also was described as being playful and having a perpetual smile and an infectious laugh, and as being warm, even tempered, generous, informal, sociable and lovable.

Alice Roosevelt:

"I do not think that I have ever known any one with the equanimity, amiability and kindness of Mr. Taft…During all that summer, I never once saw him really cross or upset. He was always beaming, genial and friendly…"[4]

Theodore Roosevelt:

"You know, I think Taft has the most lovable personality I have ever come in contact with. I almost envy a man possessing a personality like Taft's. One loves him at first sight."[5]

One Congressman remarked:

"No one, it seemed, was immune to his wholesome, warmhearted, genial charm and modest, gentle character – he was probably the most likable man to ever hold the Office of the President."[6]

A magazine editor and theologian used the following example:

"If the boat were sinking, and he could swim and you couldn't, you'd hand him your $50,000 – if you had it – saying, Give this to my wife and she'd get it."[7]

Taft's Character Gem No. 2

ENJOY LONG TERM BENEFITS FROM POSITIVE SOCIAL INTERACTION WITH OTHERS.

Taft liked to be with people rather than alone. His recreation (golf trips, fishing trips) always included a group. His amicable personality and his enjoyment of camaraderie, besides giving him personal happiness, also immensely benefitted his career. His various employers during his career liked him, respected his high ideals and character, and on a regular basis helped elevate him higher up the ladder of success.

Goodwin in *The Bully Pulpit* comments regarding Taft's time in Washington, D.C. as U.S. Solicitor General,

"Indeed, the trust and affection generated by Taft's good name made him welcome in the city's most eminent company."[8]

Taft's Character Gem No. 3

DON'T FORGET FRIENDS AND COLLEAGUES WHO HAVE HELPED YOU IN YOUR CAREER OR PERSONAL LIFE.

Taft's career was aided by many people along the way. He appreciated this assistance and wrote,

"The meanest man in the world is the man who forgets the old friends that helped him on an early day and over early difficulties."[9]

Taft's Character Gem No. 4

BENEFITS CAN BE GAINED BY LEAVING YOUR COMFORT ZONE.

Taft clearly knew his temperament was "judge-like". He went to law school in hopes of someday becoming a judge. At age 35 he was given an appointment for life as a U.S. federal judge. However, he switched career paths and resigned from this position in the judicial branch of government to join the executive branch as the first Civilian Governor of the Philippines. This led him to joining Roosevelt's cabinet as Secretary of War which eventually led to the U.S. presidency.

Taft's Character Gem No. 5
ENJOY FOOD.

Taft enjoyed food and weighed 340 pounds while president. When living in the White House he had a specially built bathtub big enough for four people.

After a horseback trip at a mountain resort, he wired Secretary of War Elihu Root:

"Stood trip well. Rode horseback twenty-five miles to five thousand foot elevation."

Root's cabled back: *"How is the horse?"*[10]

A newspaperman reflected:

"He looks like an American bison, a gentle kind one."[11]

Taft's Character Gem No. 6
IT IS OKAY TO NOT LIKE CERTAIN ASPECTS OF AMERICAN POLITICS.

Taft had little interest in politics, lacked the temperament for it and lacked political "smarts". He detested political gamesmanship and duplicity of most politicians.

Taft's Character Gem No. 7
AVOID FIGHTING, ARGUING AND CONFLICTS.

Taft enjoyed scholarly research and analysis but disliked discord and tumult. He wasn't comfortable being in the eye of a storm. Theodore Roosevelt on Taft,

"… He hates to fight unless it is necessary…There isn't a mean streak in the man's make-up."[12]

Archie Butt, his personal aide, stated he had,

"…Never known a man to dislike discord as much as the President…[he] hates to be at odds with people, and a row of any kind is repugnant to him."[13]

Taft's Character Gem No. 8
IT IS BEST TO BE METHODICAL AND METICULOUS WHEN MAKING A DECISION.

Even when not a member of the judiciary Taft worked methodically and slowly, meticulously weighing all aspects of an issue.

Character Professor William Howard Taft

Taft's Character Gem No. 9
CULTIVATE AND ENJOY HOBBIES.

Taft's passions were fishing and food. He also enjoyed automobiles, dancing, golf, tennis and horseback riding; he didn't enjoy making speeches which he compared to having surgery.

Woodrow Wilson, painting by Frank Graham Cootes, 1913

CHAPTER NINE

PERSONAL CHARACTER VALUES OF PRESIDENT AND CHARACTER PROFESSOR WOODROW WILSON

(1856-1924)
(28th U.S. President 1913-1921)

AN INTELLECT, IDEALIST and MAN of GOD, WHO HAD a COMPLEX PERSONALITY, SUCH THAT it was DIFFICULT to be HIS FRIEND

"I was never able to understand Mr. Wilson and with due deference, I doubt if you or anybody else can. He was the most extraordinary and complex character I ever encountered."[1]

—LINDLEY M. GARRISON,
Wilson's Secretary of War

"He was more than just an idealist…he brought spiritual concepts to the peace table. He was a born crusader."[2]

—HERBERT HOOVER

Searching the life of Woodrow Wilson for Red White and Blue Character Gems is bound to lead us in new directions given his strict religious upbringing and his different career path to the White House. Wilson was a man of God and of the academic world. Wilson was idealistic, somewhat similar to Jefferson. Jefferson was able to deviate from his ideals when he made the Louisiana Purchase. Wilson had a harder time being pragmatic and compromising his ideals. When Congress was debating joining the League of Nations after World War I, his refusal to compromise on a few points led to the U.S. not joining the League of Nations and also led to Wilson suffering a series of strokes from which he never fully recovered.

FAMILY BACKGROUND *and* INFLUENCES *on* WILSON'S CHARACTER

Thomas Woodrow Wilson was born in 1856 in Staunton, Virginia into a family of Presbyterian ministers and teachers. His father, Joseph Ruggles Wilson, of Irish descent, was a prominent Presbyterian minister and a strong supporter of the Confederacy during the Civil War. He was a demanding father who psychologically pressured Wilson on what to think and how to behave. Besides religion, special emphasis was placed on rhetoric and vocabulary. Wilson was never permitted to be a little boy, but rather was to always act grown-up.

A relative described Wilson's father as,

"…a cruel tease, with caustic wit and a sharp tongue, and I remember hearing my own family tell indignantly of how Cousin Woodrow suffered under his teasing."[3]

Wilson's mother, Janet ("Jessie") Woodrow was the daughter of a Scottish Presbyterian minister. She was a warm and loving mother to Wilson and they remained close throughout Wilson's life.

Wilson was a slow learner and not able to read until age eleven, perhaps because of dyslexia. Beginning at age sixteen he would learn a short hand system, again perhaps because of dyslexia.

Wilson entered Davidson College in North Carolina in 1873, but he didn't finish his first year. In 1875 he entered Princeton. He was not a great student at Princeton but enjoyed debate. After graduation from Princeton he entered the University of Virginia Law School but never finished, after suffering some type of physical or emotional trauma. He self-taught himself law, passed the Georgia Bar and practiced for a few years in Atlanta, Georgia. He soon realized the legal profession was not for him and he enrolled in 1883 in graduate school at Johns Hopkins University. He earned his Ph.D. and embarked on a career as a teacher of political science and history.

1885 was a milestone year in which Wilson published his first book *Congressional Government*, began his teaching career at Bryn Mawr College and married Ellen Louise Axson.

Ellen's father was also a Presbyterian minister. She was interested in the arts and her landscapes won several awards. The Wilsons raised three daughters, two of which had White House weddings.

Wilson moved from Bryn Mawr College to Wesleyan College in Connecticut in 1888 and then to his alma mater, Princeton, in 1890. His classes were popular with the students and his reputation in the academic world for teaching and writing rose. He stayed at Princeton for twenty years, becoming its highest paid professor and serving as its president for eight years (1902-1910).

Wilson was asked in 1910 by the leaders of the New Jersey Democratic Party to run for governor. He accepted and won in a landslide and over the next two years became a prominent national figure as a reform Democrat.

He successfully ran for president in 1912. Wilson made it clear that he was beholden to no one for his success,

"God ordained that I should be the next President of the United States. Neither you nor any other mortal could have prevented that."[4]

A year and one half into his presidency, wife Ellen died from a kidney disease. Fourteen months after Ellen's death, Wilson married Edith Bolling Galt, a widow who was a successful Washington, D.C., businesswoman.

At the conclusion of World War I, Wilson's priority was the establishment of a League of Nations so that World War I would be "the war to end all wars," "the world would be more safe for democracy," and that World War I deaths would not be in vain. Congress wanted some changes to the proposed Treaty of Versailles but Wilson refused to compromise. He chose to appeal directly to the people and went on a cross country speaking tour. The stress was too much for him and when in Pueblo, Colorado he suffered a stroke. He returned to Washington, D.C. and suffered a second, more severe stroke. He served out the final year and one half of his term as an invalid, under the care of wife Edith.

CHARACTER PROFESSOR WILSON'S RED WHITE and BLUE CHARACTER GEMS

Wilson's Character Gem No. 1

HAVE RELIGION IN YOUR LIFE.

Religion was always a part of Wilson's daily life. Wilson believed he, like all people, was an instrument of God and God was using him to do virtuous things. Wilson is the only president to be buried in a church (Washington National Cathedral).

Wilson's Character Gem No. 2

LIVE A VIRTUOUS, MORALISTIC AND RIGHTEOUS LIFE.

Do God's work. Wilson had uncompromising integrity at all times, which was never questioned even by his rivals.

Wilson's Character Gem No. 3

LIFE IS ALL ABOUT IDEALS. ESTABLISH IDEALS; LIVE UP TO YOUR IDEALS.

With his intellectual and scholarly background, Wilson brought to Princeton and then to the presidency high ideals on how things ought to be.

"It is not men that interest or disturb me primarily; it is ideas. Ideas live; men die."[5]

When his "ideals" clashed with "reality", he occasionally was forced to compromise to some extent and accept a somewhat less solution, but more often he dug in his heels and fervently fought without compromising.

"I am not the kind that considers compromise when I once take a position."[6]

Wilson's Character Gem No. 4
ALLOW CHILDREN TO HAVE A CHILDHOOD.

In reflecting on his upbringing, Wilson regretted that his father pressured him prematurely to act grown-up.

"I suppose that nothing is more painful in the recollections of some of us than the efforts that were made to make us like grown-up people."[7]

Wilson's Character Gem No. 5
BE INDEPENDENT
AND BEHOLDEN TO NO ONE.

Wilson was not generally a "joiner", he had few friends and was proud that he was beholden to no one. Upon becoming president, he boldly told his Democratic party leaders,

"Before we proceed, I wish it clearly understood that I owe you nothing."[8]

Wilson's Character Gem No. 6
DO GREAT DEEDS FOR THE BENEFIT OF OTHERS AND NOT PERSONAL GAIN.

Wilson was not interested in personal gain from his success; rather altruistic service for others was his goal.

Wilson's Character Gem No. 7
PURSUE AND ENJOY A SCHOLARLY AND ACADEMIC LIFESTYLE.

Wilson was a college professor for eighteen years and a college president for eight years. His classes were popular with the students for his "witting performances". At one time, he was the highest paid professor at Princeton.

Wilson's Character Gem No. 8
YOU BENEFIT FROM AN EFFECTIVE USE OF VOCABULARY.

Wilson's father was an eloquent minister and ingrained in Wilson the importance and effectiveness of expressing his thoughts. Debate was a principal activity while at college. Wilson also became editor of the Princeton school newspaper. Throughout his life Wilson wrote numerous well-received books and essays. He also wrote love letters to his wife Edith. In addition to his writings, he became a persuasive and inspirational teacher and orator.

Wilson's Character Gem No. 9
WHEN APPROPRIATE, USE POWER AND AUTHORITY TO DO VIRTUOUS DEEDS.

Wilson chose to leave academia and use his power for virtue and righteousness. Upon obtaining power and authority, he used it boldly (at times, defiantly).

Wilson's Character Gem No. 10
DON'T BE A LAWYER.

Wilson found law to be a boring profession and compared it to eating hash every day.

"...the Law, gets as monotonous as the other immortal article of food, Hash, when served with such endless frequency."[9]

Wilson's Character Gem No. 11
PLAYING GOLF MAY NOT HELP.

President Wilson played golf almost every day for health reasons as recommended by his doctor. This may not have helped to extend his life as he died at age sixty-seven after several strokes.

Wilson's Character Gem No. 12
CULTIVATE AND ENJOY HOBBIES.

Wilson enjoyed golf (almost every day when president on doctor's orders; 1,200 rounds in 6 ½ years), movies, automobiles, baseball, bicycling and poetry.

Coolidge with wife Grace (nicknamed "Sunshine") and dog Prudence Prim, 1924

CHAPTER TEN

PERSONAL CHARACTER VALUES OF PRESIDENT AND CHARACTER PROFESSOR CALVIN COOLIDGE
(1872-1933)
(30th U.S. President 1923-1929)

"SILENT CAL", THE NON-ROARING PURITAN PRESIDENT DURING *the* ROARING 1920'S ERA *of* SPEAKEASIES *and* FLAPPERS

"A Puritan in Babylon."[1]
—WILLIAM ALLEN WHITE

"Cal Coolidge seldom smiles, hardly even does any hand shaking, and has a reputation that his word is as good as gold."[2]
—A REPORTER FOR THE *NEW YORK WORLD*, 1919

"Coolidge is outwardly neither impressive nor expressive, and looking at him therefore is rather wasting time…He admittedly lacks all oratorical power in addressing a crowd and all personal magnetism in meeting an individual…Yet for some years, he has been the surest vote-getter in Massachusetts."[3]
—A REPORTER FOR THE *NEW YORK WORLD*, 1920

Coolidge with the great Walter Johnson, 1925

Calvin Coolidge was a fifth generation Vermonter. That basically tells it all. He was proud of being from Vermont and possessing the values and temperament of his Puritan ancestors and his Vermont neighbors.

Although Coolidge earned a law degree and practiced law for a while, his real profession was being a grass roots politician and rising slowly through the ranks by winning election after election. His popularity and so his electability never ceased. He refused to run for a third presidential term even though he was all but assured of victory.

This popularity of Coolidge continues to baffle many historians because he possessed little of the personality traits and skills of most all successful politicians. Journalist Sherwin Cook wrote,

> *"Coolidge's unimpressive physique, his reticence, his lack of florid speech, his utter want of social attributes, his entire aloofness, are proverbial. How could such a man ever have been elected to a municipal council?"*[4]

New York Governor and 1928 U.S. presidential candidate Al Smith, after the death of Coolidge, wrote that Coolidge was a member,

> *"...in the class of Presidents who were distinguished for character more than for heroic achievements. His great task was to restore the dignity and prestige of the Presidency when it had reached the lowest ebb in our history, and to afford in a time of extravagance and waste, a shining example of the simple and honest virtues which came down to him from his New England ancestors. These are no small achievements, and history will not forget them."*[5]

BRIEF BACKGROUND *and* INFLUENCES *on* COOLIDGE'S CHARACTER

John Calvin Coolidge, Jr. was born in 1872 in Plymouth Notch, Vermont, a tiny hamlet in the eastern foothills of the Green Mountains. He was the fifth generation Coolidge of Plymouth Notch, mostly all farmers and New England Puritans in outlook and spirit. The temperament was serious, stoic and cautious.

> *"The Coolidge family shared the attitudes common to the region; the Puritan piety, the esteem of hard work and thrift..."*[6]

Coolidge's father, John Calvin Coolidge, Sr. (1845-1926), was one of the more prosperous farmers. Along with owning his farm, he owned a general store and later became active in politics, rising to Vermont state senator. Numerous historians have concluded that a prime motivating force in Coolidge's life was to garner the approval and respect of his father.

Coolidge's mother, Victoria Moor Coolidge (1846-1885), also was a descendant of Plymouth Notch farmers. She died when Coolidge was only twelve years old. Reflecting back when an adult, Coolidge wrote,

> *"The greatest grief that can come to a boy came to me. Life was never to seem the same again."*[7]

He always carried a picture of her and it was with him when he died at age sixty.

Coolidge began his education in a one room schoolhouse, but for high school moved away from the farm to Ludlow, Vermont to attend Black River Academy. Upon graduation, he attended college at Amherst in Northampton, Massachusetts. After college, he studied law as an apprentice in a small Northampton law firm. In 1905 he married the beautiful Grace Goodhue (1879-1957), who had graduated from the University of Vermont and became a teacher of handicapped children. Dissimilar to Coolidge she was gregarious, talkative, smiled and laughed. As First Lady, she offset her husband's lack of social skills. The Secret Service nicknamed her "Sunshine." They had two sons, John (1906-2000), who graduated from Amherst College and had a successful business career, and Calvin Jr. (1908-1924), whose death from blood poisoning while Coolidge was president devasted Coolidge.

Coolidge came to national prominence in 1919 when as governor of Massachusetts he responded after much deliberation to a Boston police strike by calling up the National Guard to end the lawlessness and restore peace and safety. After serving two terms as U.S. president he declined to run for reelection in 1928 even though he was all but sure of winning.

In 1933 *The New York Times* wrote,

> "The prestige of Coolidge was so great at the end of his second term [as President] that the leaders of his party wished to override the tradition that no President should have a third term. It was with difficulty that President Coolidge prevented his enthusiastic re-nomination by the Republican National Convention in 1928."[8]

In addition to the death of his mother when Coolidge was twelve, his sister died when Coolidge was fifteen and both his sixteen year old son, Calvin Jr. and his father died while he was president. Each death had a serious lasting emotional impact on Coolidge. The death of Calvin Jr. was a tragic, life-changing event for Coolidge. Severe depression set in, from which Coolidge may have never recovered. His wife remembered he "lost his zest for living." Coolidge wrote,

> "When he [Calvin Jr.] went, the power and glory of the Presidency went with him."[9]

CHARACTER PROFESSOR COOLIDGE'S RED WHITE *and* BLUE CHARACTER GEMS

Coolidge's Character Gem No. 1
SILENCE IS GOLDEN.

Hanging on the wall in Coolidge's Northampton, Massachusetts' home:

*"A wise old owl lived in an oak.
The more he saw, the less he spoke,
the less he spoke the more he heard.
Why can't we be like that old bird?"*[10]

Silent Cal was painfully shy as a youth and was extremely uncomfortable around strangers. He was a loner and never became a "people person". He never enjoyed any type or level of banter with anyone. He spoke in dry direct short sentences. He was of the strong opinion that silence avoids stirring up situations that might otherwise not exist.

"I have never been hurt by what I have not said."[11]

"[he was]…an eloquent listener, one who could be silent in five languages."[12]

His wife Grace, when asked about her own vivaciousness, replied,

"Well, I have to talk for two."[13]

At first Coolidge's silence made him a subject of ridicule. Later his silence was regarded as a supremely positive trait and became a legend.

Coolidge's Character Gem No. 2
ADOPT A STABLE, NON-GLITZY LIFESTYLE.

Coolidge left the Vermont rural community of his ancestors but maintained the values of his Vermont and Puritan roots throughout his entire life.

Renowned journalist Michael Hennessy,

"…people liked him because he kept his word and was scrupulously honest. He inherited from his Vermont ancestors their characteristics of plain living and high thinking, taciturnity and humor."[14]

Coolidge's Character Gem No. 3
LIFE IS NOT JUST ABOUT HAVING A GOOD TIME, BUT RATHER EVERY AMERICAN HAS A DUTY TO HELP OTHERS.

Unselfishly, Coolidge chose a career of public service. He had strong feelings instilled by his father that everyone has an obligation to assist others. The voters understood this and he won election after election.

Biographer Donald R. McCoy wrote,

"Coolidge's reason for being in politics was that the citizen had an obligation to serve. It was his duty to God and society."[15]

Similarly, biographer Gamaliel Bradford writes of the overriding New England temperament of duty to others which Coolidge followed,

"The truth is, it was not in his temperament to enjoy glory or anything else. That temperament was the inherited, cumulative, aggravated temperament of New England, in which the sense of duty is the overriding force, and an uneasy conscience suggests that we are not in this world mainly to have a good time, or even to have a good time at all, but for some higher purpose."[16]

Coolidge's Character Gem No. 4

REDUCE STRESS BY SIMPLY DOING THE RIGHT THING.

Robert Ferrell in his book Calvin Coolidge writes:

"There was a remarkable simplicity about Coolidge that is still attractive...He had the ability to peel off the layers of confusion and complexity that seem to attach to almost all questions not merely of politics but of life...There was elemental quality about him that enabled him to analyze. It helped him to choose his courses and pursue them."[17]

He was able to "peel off" the layers of confusion because his moral compass made his personal and public life easier.

Coolidge's Character Gem No. 5

CHARACTER IMPROVEMENT IS MORE IMPORTANT THAN MATERIALISTIC GAIN.

Coolidge was not driven by a need for wealth. To Coolidge,

"Prosperity is only an instrument to be used, not a deity to be worshipped."[18]

"We do not need more material development, we need spiritual development. We do not need more intellectual power, we need more moral power. We do not need more knowledge, we need more character…We do not need more of the things that are seen, we need more of the things that are unseen. It is on this side of life that it is desirable to put emphasis at the present time. If that side be strengthened, the other side will take care of itself."[19]

On another occasion he wrote,

"We must forever realize that material rewards are limited and in a sense, they are only incidental, but the development of character is unlimited and is the only essential. The measure of success is not the quantity of merchandise, but the quality of manhood which is produced."[20]

Coolidge's Character Gem No. 6
MATTERS OF IMPORTANCE ARE USUALLY OBTAINED STEP BY STEP, NOT BY A QUICK FIX.

Coolidge on several occasions recited the following verse, which coincides with his steady rise up the ladder of success:

"Heaven is not reached at a single bound;
We build the ladder by which we rise
From the lowly earth to the vaulted skies,
And we mount to its summit round by round."[21]

Coolidge's Character Gem No. 7
FOCUS ON WHAT IS IN FRONT OF YOU.

Coolidge thought everyone should do their days work, and not worry and fret about what might happen in the future. He felt people wasted too much time and energy working themselves into a frenzy about possible situations that never arose. He similarly felt people make mistakes when they act prematurely, far in advance of when action is proper and prudent.

"If you see ten troubles coming down the road, you can be sure that nine will run into the ditch before they reach you..."[22]

One reporter observed after the Boston police strike,

"He had the experience to know when to act, but more important, when not to intrude."[23]

Coolidge's Character Gem No. 8
APPRECIATE NATURE AND THE RURAL COUNTRYSIDE.

Coolidge was proud of his heritage and of a rural lifestyle and values,

"Vermont is my birthright. Here one gets close to nature, in the mountains, in the brooks…My folks are happy and contented. They belong to themselves, live within their incomes and fear no man."[24]

"I stay all the time in the open air, which has been the real source of the benefits I have received. I therefore should like to commend that source to you. If you could find something like fishing that would keep you out of doors, I hope you might receive a like benefit."[25]

"Country life does not always have breath, but it has depth. It is neither artificial nor superficial…"[26]

Coolidge's Character Gem No. 9
BE FRUGAL – SAVE, SAVE, SAVE FOR A RAINY DAY!

Frugality was a cornerstone for Coolidge throughout his life. Debt to him was evil. He penny-pinched and saved for a rainy day even when a poorly paid local official. His father had taught him that waste was a "moral wrong." He delayed marriage until his income rose. When he left the White House, he moved back to the humble two-family house he had lived in before in Northampton, Massachusetts.

"There is no dignity quite so impressive, and no independence quite so important, as living within your means."[27]

Coolidge closely managed his expenses.

"I regard a good budget as among the noblest monuments of virtue."[28]

Coolidge's Character Gem No. 10

IT IS WISE TO BE CAUTIOUS; BETTER TO BE RIGHT THAN QUICK.

Coolidge was a disciplined man and did everything slowly and cautiously, weighing the pros and cons, the costs and benefits. He was never impulsive. According to the *The New York Times*,

"He listened, he assimilated and he waited until there appeared what seemed the soundest course."[29]

A Boston banker official, after the settlement of the police strike which made Coolidge famous, wrote to a friend:

"Coolidge never is quick on the trigger, but he keeps his mind right on the problem, and it is generally more important…to be right than quick."[30]

A neighbor of Coolidge used a baseball analogy to describe Coolidge's cautious approach:

"You see, he never makes mistakes. He has the limitations of his Vermont Yankee hereditary. He was born cautious. All great men make mistakes, probably more mistakes than anything else. Three times out of five that great men come to bat, they strike out. The other two times are home runs though Calvin never takes a chance and strikes out, and never hits a home run. A base hit is his limit. He'll make that every time, to do him justice."[31]

Coolidge's Character Gem No. 11

PERSISTENCE AND HARD WORK ARE OMNIPOTENT.

Coolidge was successful as a result of hard work and persistence.

"Nothing in this world can take the place of persistence. Talent will not…Genius will not…Education will not…Persistence and determination alone are omnipotent…the slogan 'Press On' has solved and always will solve the problems of the human race."[32]

Coolidge's Character Gem No. 12

CULTIVATE AND ENJOY HOBBIES.

When asked about his hobbies, Coolidge seriously replied "running for office" (he ran for elective office nineteen times, winning seventeen). He also enjoyed the great outdoors and a rural lifestyle, baseball, cigars and dogs *("Any man who does not like dogs and want them about does not deserve to be in the White House")*.[33]

Hoover with his dog King Tut, 1928

CHAPTER ELEVEN

PERSONAL CHARACTER VALUES OF PRESIDENT AND CHARACTER PROFESSOR HERBERT HOOVER
(1874-1964)
(31st U.S. President 1929-1933)

CALLED "THE MASTER *of* EMERGENCIES" and "THE GREAT HUMANITARIAN" YET TODAY DOESN'T GET ADEQUATE RESPECT *or* PRAISE

"Few if any Americans have dedicated more of their lives to the service of others than Hoover. A wealthy man by age 40, he turned his back on opportunities to earn more — and dissipated much of what he had gained — to devote himself to humanitarian work."[1]

—DAVID FRUM,
Senior Editor at *The Atlantic*, 2017

"Once upon a time my political opponents honored me as possessing the fabulous intellectual and economic power by which I created a worldwide depression all by myself."[2]

—HERBERT HOOVER

Hoover fishing, 1929

With Herbert Hoover we again have a unique career path to the White House, in that he was a mining engineer. We also have another American success story of a poor orphan who by hard work became overwhelmingly successful. Hoover retired at a young age from the business world and devoted his life to public service. He donated much of his wealth to charity. His Quaker upbringing was an important factor in the character values that put him on the path to financial success and eventually to the White House.

FAMILY BACKGROUND *and* INFLUENCES *on* HOOVER'S CHARACTER

Bert (or Bertie) Hoover, as he was called, was born into a poor Quaker family and community in the small town of West Branch, Iowa. His father, Jesse, of English, Swiss and German ancestry, was a friendly energetic blacksmith and small shop owner who died when Bert was six. His mother, Huldah, of Irish and English ancestry, was a serious-minded disciplinarian and an active religious speaker and teacher within the Quaker church. She died when Bert was nine. Bert and his brother and sister were separated and Bert ended up being adopted by his Quaker uncle in Newberg, Oregon, Dr. John Minthorn, a stern and stoic doctor. Life was serious in the Minthorn household and Bert was lonely, repressed and unhappy. He dropped out of school when thirteen and began work in a real estate office. He attended night school.

On the positive side, Oregon imbued in Bert a love of the outdoors.

> *"He grew to love Oregon's vast expanses of forests, mountains and streams. He found a greater variety of fish than in Iowa, and he learned the art of fly fishing."*[3]

Bert's Quaker ancestry gave him a work ethic, and taught him charity and service to others, thrift, modesty, individualism and self-reliance. Being pacifists, no military toys or games were allowed.

Bert's big break came when he heard about a new college being built by Leland Stanford in northern California. One of the initial professors was a Quaker known to Dr. Minthorn. Bert became a member of Stanford's first graduating class, having consistently worked odd jobs on campus to pay his way. He also played for one year on the baseball team. His degree was in mining engineering.

At Stanford, Bert met his wife, Lou Henry, who also was of Quaker heritage and was the first female geology major at Stanford. The love of his life, she was beautiful, bright, athletic, with a bubbly personality. She and Bert shared a love of the outdoors, horses, hunting, fishing, hiking and camping. Lou was equally adept in the wilderness or dancing in the ballroom.

After graduation from Stanford, Hoover spent a couple of years in the California gold fields before joining a London based mining company that sent him in 1897 to Australia and then in 1899 to China. During his business career, Bert had offices worldwide including in San Francisco, New York City, St. Petersburg, Paris, London, Melbourne, Johannesburg, Rangoon and Tianjin (China). By age forty, Hoover retired independently wealthy and spent the remaining fifty years of his life doing public service.

The start of World War I accelerated Bert's transition from the business world to public service. He and Lou were in Europe and led the effort to evacuate 120,000 Americans who wanted to flee harm's way. Bert's efforts in this project led subsequently to a series of other significant public service assignments and hence the reputation as "The Master of Emergencies" and "The Great Humanitarian."

Bert and Lou had two sons. Both sons accompanied their parents in their worldwide globetrotting experiences.

CHARACTER PROFESSOR HOOVER'S RED WHITE *and* BLUE CHARACTER GEMS

Hoover's Character Gem No. 1
IT IS OKAY TO BE A "GREGARIOUS HERMIT."

Hoover had conflicting emotional needs. He was shy, aloof, somewhat awkward socially and an intensely private person who loved the solitude of nature. Fishing was his escape, where he found peace and quiet.

However, at the same time, he also needed companionship. He would venture into the forests, but always with people. He was called a "gregarious hermit" by journalist William Hand,

"The President has a very great reputation for loving solitude… his delight in going off into the deep woods and being by himself. The fact is that when he goes into the deep woods, he goes virtually always with companions."[4]

His wife Lou:

"He always wants to have people around him. The more he has, the happier he is."[5]

Hoover's Character Gem No. 2

ORGANIZATIONAL SKILLS CAN BOTH SOLVE EXISTING PROBLEMS AND PREVENT FUTURE PROBLEMS.

Hoover loved nothing better than to be called upon in a crisis to use his skills for organization and administration. Senator Frederic Walcott:

"Mr. Hoover is a perfect wonder…one of the most remarkable men I have ever met…a perfect genius for organization."[6]

Hoover's organizational skills led to success as The Great Humanitarian, which led to becoming president.

Hoover's Character Gem No. 3

ENJOY NATURE AND THE GREAT OUTDOORS.

Hoover was a life-long outdoorsman. He and Lou especially loved the Monterey Peninsula near their Palo Alto home and their rural retreat in southern Oregon. Fishing, both freshwater and saltwater, was Hoover's first love. Hoover was:

"…rarely at ease when not wielding a fishing pole."[7]

Hoover,

"Fishing is much more than fish. It is the great occasion when we return to the fine simplicity of our forefathers."[8]

Hoover's Character Gem No. 4
FINANCIALLY ASSIST YOUR FAMILY MEMBERS.

Hoover was a generous man. He assisted his siblings financially immediately upon his employment as a mining engineer. He quietly gave to family and friends in need throughout his life.

Hoover's Character Gem No. 5
APPRECIATE AND LOVE THE U.S.A.

Hoover and his wife lived and worked around the world (including Australia, China, Burma, Russia, France and England). This reinforced Hoover's love of the U.S. as the land of freedom.

Hoover's Character Gem No. 6
THE U.S.A. IS STILL THE LAND OF OPPORTUNITY THROUGH HARD WORK.

What was true for Benjamin Franklin was true for Hoover one hundred fifty years later. Both started with nothing and achieved success through character, initiative and hard work. Upon Hoover's death, The New York Times wrote:

"…*his own life proof of the America dream through achievement, effort, not grant.*"[9]

Hoover's Character Gem No. 7
VOLUNTEER.

Hoover preached and put into practice his strong belief that private solutions to problems exist, not just governmental programs. Hoover was a strong proponent of private solutions to problems, where people and private (non-governmental) associations worked together to solve problems. His Quaker heritage was one in which Quakers voluntarily helped each other.

Hoover's Character Gem No. 8
MAKE A DIFFERENCE AND FIND PERSONAL SATISFACTION BY SUPPORTING HUMANITARIAN CAUSES.

With his Quaker sense of duty to others, Hoover devoted the last fifty years of his life to helping others. The whole world applauded his food relief efforts in war torn Europe.

Upon Hoover's death a friend, Neil MacNeil wrote:

"A great American has ended a brilliant career of service to his fellow man. Above all, he was a humanitarian. He fed more people and saved more lives than other man in history."[10]

Hoover and his wife generously supported numerous charities by giving of their own funds and by spearheading fund drives. One main cause was the Boys' Clubs of America, of which Hoover became Chairman.

Hoover's Character Gem No. 9

INTEGRATE INTO YOUR LIFE MANY OF THE QUAKER VALUES SUCH AS SELF-RELIANCE, HARD WORK, CHARITY AND SERVICE TO OTHERS.

Hoover was raised in a Quaker community by both his natural parents and then adopted parents. His wife, Lou, was similarly of Quaker heritage. Quaker ethics stayed with him throughout his life, especially individualism and self-reliance, charity and service to others, the benefits from hard work, and the benefits from a simple, non-ostentatious and uncomplicated lifestyle.

Hoover's Character Gem No. 10

IT'S OKAY NOT TO LIKE VERY MANY POLITICIANS.

Hoover didn't enjoy politics and didn't like very many politicians. He once remarked that there was one congressman who was proof of a negative I.Q. Hoover simply wasn't a politician, but rather an engineer turned public servant.

Hoover's Character Gem No. 11

CULTIVATE AND ENJOY HOBBIES.

Hoover's passion was fishing. He also enjoyed camping and the great outdoors, baseball, dancing, and his German Shepherd King Tut.

Franklin Roosevelt at the Yalta Summit 1945 with Churchill and Stalin

Eleanor Roosevelt, 1949

CHAPTER TWELVE

PERSONAL CHARACTER VALUES OF PRESIDENT AND CHARACTER PROFESSOR FRANKLIN DELANO ROOSEVELT
(1882 – 1945)
(32nd U.S. President 1933 – 1945)

100% PURE POLITICIAN WHO LED A SUCCESSFUL YET TROUBLED LIFE

"…the most complicated human being I have ever known."[1]
—FRANCES PERKINS,
FDR's Secretary of Labor

"He is the truest friend; he has the farthest vision; he is the greatest man I've ever known."[2]
—WINSTON CHURCHILL,
at the close of the Casablanca Conference during World War II

Roosevelt with wife Eleanor and children Anna and James, 1908

Despite his family's wealth, Franklin Delano Roosevelt led a complicated and problematic life. Of course the watershed event in his life was contracting polio and being paralyzed from the waist down from age thirty-nine. Rejecting his mother's wishes that he become somewhat a recluse in his New York City mansion, FDR was determined to live as normal and productive a life as humanly possible. He remained positive and optimistic, with a smile on his face. Rather than garner sympathy he did his best to hide his handicap from the public. The result is that he became America's longest serving president, the president who fought the Great Depression and the president that led the U.S. war effort against Germany, Italy and Japan.

The marriage of Franklin and Eleanor evolved in numerous ways over the years. While mutual love was lost and never regained, mutual respect and caring continued.

Character Professor Franklin Delano Roosevelt

FAMILY BACKGROUND *and* INFLUENCES *on* FDR'S CHARACTER

Franklin Delano Roosevelt was born in the Hudson Valley village of Hyde Park, New York, in 1882 to a wealthy and socially prominent family made famous by cousin, Theodore Roosevelt. Both of FDR's parents, James, of Dutch ancestry and Sara Delano, of English ancestry, came from wealth. James was lawyer trained but instead focused on his coal and transportation businesses. Sara at age twenty-six became the second wife of James, at age fifty-two.

    Father James had a heart attack when FDR was eight and his health steadily declined until his death when FDR was eighteen. FDR was Sara's only child. She was strong willed with a controlling, domineering personality, and FDR was the focus of her life. Some historians suggest Sara was the most important person in FDR's life. Her comfort, security and money gave FDR confidence.

    FDR grew up on a large estate, traveled to Europe frequently, attended the prestigious private school, Groton, and then Harvard. After father James died, Sara moved to Cambridge to be close to FDR. At Groton and Harvard FDR was just an average student, although his senior year he was editor-in-chief of the school newspaper, the *Harvard Crimson*. After Harvard FDR attended Columbia Law School and again was just an average student.

    While at Harvard in 1902 FDR met Eleanor Roosevelt, a distant cousin. Sara tried to prevent the marriage and took FDR on a Caribbean cruise in the hope that he would end their engagement. FDR and Eleanor married in 1905 with Theodore Roosevelt giving the bride away. Sara built adjoining townhouses in New York City for the married couple and herself. FDR never had a home of his own until he moved into the White House.

Eleanor, being a "Roosevelt", also was born into a wealthy family but had a tragic childhood. Her mother died in 1892 when she was eight, a brother died the next year and her father, (Theodore's brother) was an alcoholic who died the following year while confined to a sanitarium. Eleanor was raised by her maternal grandmother with the help of other relatives.

Eleanor and FDR had six children, with one dying in infancy. Living next door to the domineering Sara meant that Sara ran both households. Eleanor once commented that the children were more her mother-in-law's children than hers.

Eleanor was plain looking, shy and reserved, but intelligent, warm and compassionate.

Sometime around 1914 FDR started an extra-marital affair with Lucy Mercer, secretary to Eleanor. Eleanor learned of the affair in 1918 when she discovered love letters in FDR's luggage. FDR agreed to never see Lucy again and the marriage continued in a fashion. Eleanor and FDR lived apart but continued to have a type of "caring partnership" in which Eleanor assisted FDR's political career and FDR assisted Eleanor's social and humanitarian projects.

In 1921 at age thirty-nine FDR was stricken with polio. He would for the rest of his life wear heavy steel braces on both legs. Even with a cane, he could not walk very far without assistance. He spent his life in a wheelchair. Some historians point out that the combination of losing Lucy Mercer and contracting polio made FDR less arrogant and more sensitive to the concerns of others.

In the 1920's, Eleanor's companionship was replaced by FDR's new secretary, Missy LeHand. H.W. Brands, in his biography of FDR,

"For two decades Missy LeHand had scarcely left Roosevelt's side. She served as secretary, gatekeeper, surrogate wife, second mother, adoring partisan, loving friend. She gave up any semblance of a normal life to serve him. He knew it, and he loved her for it."[3]

In 1941 she suffered a major stroke and never fully recovered. FDR changed his will to provide her financial support in the event he died before her, which was not to be the case.

In 1932 FDR was elected president in the midst of the Great Depression which lasted until World War II.

During World War II, FDR closely collaborated with Winston Churchill and Joseph Stalin to lead the war effort and establish the goals for post-World War II Europe and Asia. Eleanor traveled throughout the U.S. during FDR's Presidency and was his "eyes and ears". They continued their warm and friendly partnership-like marriage until FDR's death shortly after the start of his fourth term in 1945.

HEAR YE! HEAR YE!

CHARACTER PROFESSOR FDR'S RED WHITE *and* BLUE CHARACTER GEMS

FDR's Character Gem No. 1
STOP COMPLAINING!

From age thirty-nine FDR was paralyzed from the waist down from polio. Although he was for a period of time depressed, he never complained or sought sympathy.

FDR's Character Gem No. 2
NEVER GIVE UP! HAVE GUTS AND DETERMINATION TO OVERCOME ANY PHYSICAL HANDICAPS, SETBACKS OR DESPAIR.

FDR overcame depression and learned to live his life without the ability to walk. He could not move his hips and could stand only because of fourteen-pound steel braces. He knew that to continue his political career he would have to "walk" in some fashion in certain situations. Through guts and determination he endured great pain and taught himself to walk short distances by lunging.

Brands described this struggle,

"Because his hip and thigh muscles didn't have the strength and coordination to swing the braces, he had to employ the muscles of his abdomen and lower back. He would prop himself on two crutches and one leg awhile, with a lean and a twisting heave

of his pelvis, he threw the other leg forward. After months of strenuous practice he managed to develop a kind of rhythm, which made his gait resemble a walk in tempo if in little else. Yet he never became really stable, and he kept to his wheelchair except when something extraordinary dictated that he stand."[4]

The 1924 Democratic political convention was held in Madison Square Garden and FDR was given the opportunity to make a major speech. Smith described FDR's guts and determination,

"Then came the moment when FDR would have to walk alone: the moment he had been practicing for. James handed him his second crutch, and he began moving slowly toward the podium unassisted. Marion Dickerman held her breath and prayed. 'It seemed like an hour', she remembered. Frances Perkins, sitting near the platform, recalled that no one in the Garden seemed to breathe. Eight thousand delegates, alternates and spectators watched spell-bound as FDR fought his way across the stage, the personification of courage, defying pain with every forward thrust of his heavily braced legs. When he finally reached the podium, unable to wave for fear of falling but flashing that famous smile, head thrown back, shoulders high, the Garden erupted with a thunderous ovation. Delegates rose to their feet and cheered for three minutes, admiration tinged with awe at the dramatic performance they had witnessed."[5]

FDR's Character Gem No. 3
SMILE, BE UPBEAT, OPTIMISTIC.

FDR met everyone with a smile, as if they were a friend. Churchill said to meet FDR was like opening your first bottle of champagne.

His son Elliott said,

"His father was the model of cheerfulness" and *"he invariably woke in a high good humor, ready and eager to tackle anything the day might bring...I do not remember a breakfast time when there wasn't a smile on his lips and in his eyes."*[6]

Eleanor's special friend, Lorena Hickok,

"I never knew anyone who had a better sense of humor than Franklin Roosevelt."[7]

Eleanor once remarked to a friend when discussing FDR,

"Remember, the nicest men in the world are those who always keep something of the little boy in them."[8]

He had no fear of the future. He had extreme confidence in himself and in America. His confidence and optimism were contagious to all he met.

FDR's Character Gem No. 4
DAILY RELAXATION IS CRITICAL; MAYBE EVEN HAVE A COCKTAIL.

FDR knew that daily relaxation would help restore his energy and improve his mental outlook. While in the White House, FDR would hold his daily "Children's Hour", when he would mix cocktails and no business would be discussed. It was a time of fun, silliness and gossip. FDR was a people person, he needed companionship and never wanted to be alone.

FDR's Character Gem No. 5
DON'T BE THIN-SKINNED.

FDR could make fun of his own shortcomings.

FDR's Character Gem No. 6
DO YOUR BEST, THAT IS ALL THAT ANYONE CAN ASK.

FDR was not a worrier. Each night he slept soundly because of his lifelong philosophy that all a person can do is try and give it your best.

FDR's Character Gem No. 7
BE A GOOD COMMUNICATOR.

FDR was a great communicator, in one-on-one conversations with visitors, in small groups such as committee meetings and in public speaking to crowds. He had a talent of simplifying complex issues and spoke with a casual, cheerful and easy manner. He put people at ease. He never tried to browbeat or intimidate.

Frances Perkins remarked,

"As he talked, his head would nod and his hands would move in simple, natural, comfortable gestures. His face would smile and light up as though he was actually sitting on the front porch or in the parlor with them."[9]

Will Rogers said,

"The President explained banking issues so well that even bankers understood it."[10]

FDR's Character Gem No. 8
BE PRACTICAL.

He was practical, pragmatic and not idealistic or theoretical. He didn't focus on and was not bound by any ideology. Brands,

"He was a politician, not an ideologue; he served people, not causes."[11]

FDR's Character Gem No. 9

IT IS OKAY TO SHIELD YOUR INNER EMOTIONS.

FDR created a protective impenetrable façade and kept his emotions to himself. He had no close friends with whom he was intimate and never expressed true inner feelings.

His son James said,

"Of what was inside him…Father talked with no one."[12]

He avoided uncomfortable personal situations.

Secretary of Labor Frances Perkins,

"He dropped the curtain over himself. He never told you, or anyone else, just what was going on inside his mind – inside his emotions – inside his real intentions in life…I think he never intended to reveal himself."[13]

People aware of FDR's emotional isolation, describe FDR as an actor who never left the stage.

FDR's Character Gem No. 10
ALWAYS STAY CALM.

FDR's reaction to any great event was always to be completely calm. Eleanor said he was like an iceberg.

In 1932, after an assassination attempt, Raymond Moley wrote: *"Roosevelt was simply himself – easy, confident, poised, to all appearances unnerved… I confess that I have never in my life seen anything more magnificent than Roosevelt's calm that night…"*[14]

FDR's Character Gem No. 11
HAVE ENERGY! BE PROACTIVE; BE A "DOER".

FDR was energetic to an extreme, a man who moved forward and got things done. He didn't make excuses; he didn't look for others to do something; he didn't do things halfway; he took action and didn't cease until his goal was accomplished.

FDR's Character Gem No. 12
BE FLEXIBLE AND WILLING TO EXPERIMENT.

If FDR didn't have the answer to a complex problem, he was willing to take risks, even if failure was a possibility.

"Take a method and try it…if it fails, admit it and try another. But, above all, try something."[15]

"I have no expectation of making a hit every time I come to bat…what I seek is the highest possible batting average."[16]

FDR's Character Gem No. 13

DON'T BROWBEAT OR TRY TO HUMILIATE, INSTEAD PERHAPS BE FRIENDLY AND MAYBE SLIGHTLY A LITTLE CRAFTY AND SLY TO ACCOMPLISH YOUR GOALS.

FDR preferred to use charm, wit and friendly banter.

James MacGregor Burns called him,

"a lion and a fox."[17]

When he met a visitor, he always reacted "agreeable" without "agreeing". He couldn't discipline his children and he couldn't fire anyone including the White House cook even though the food was *"drab, dull and overcooked"*[18] (Truman promptly fired her). He told jokes and treated employees and visitors as friends, using their first names.

FDR's Character Gem No. 14

CONTINUE YOUR STRONG BOND WITH YOUR PARENTS.

FDR and his mother Sara remained close throughout their lives.

HEAR YE! HEAR YE!

FDR's Character Gem No. 15

BE FLEXIBLE TO IMPROVE
YOUR MARRIAGE AND FRIENDSHIPS.

FDR was able to establish a "partnership" of respect and caring out of a broken marriage. FDR and Eleanor each lived separate lives but each continued to regularly assist and give support to each other. Each cared about the happiness of the other.

FDR's Character Gem No. 16

CULTIVATE AND ENJOY HOBBIES.

FDR enjoyed fishing, sailing and the sea, movies, small stakes poker, swimming, stamp collecting (his entire life from age eight) and his Scottish terrier Fala.

Harry Truman, while President

CHAPTER THIRTEEN

PERSONAL CHARACTER VALUES OF PRESIDENT AND CHARACTER PROFESSOR HARRY S. TRUMAN
(1884-1972)
(33rd U.S. President 1945-1953)

THE "COMMON MAN'S COMMON MAN" WHO WAS CONFRONTED WITH, *and* DECISIVELY MADE, MONUMENTAL DECISIONS ONE AFTER ANOTHER

When asked if he was an "average man", Truman replied "Well, what is wrong with being the average man?"[1]

"…he proved that the ordinary American is capable of grandeur. And that a President can be a human being…"[2]
—JOURNALIST MARY MCGRORY
in the *Washington Star* after Truman's death

Truman and wife Bess and daughter Margaret, 1934

Truman with General MacArthur in 1950, who Truman famously fired in 1951

Harry Truman's life story is that of a common American man from the Midwest ending up in the White House and doing a solid job as president. Prior to becoming president there wasn't anything special about Harry Truman. He didn't go to college and wasn't much of a success in anything. The watershed event in his life was going to France during World War I. In the Army he gained confidence and equally important he met James Pendergast, nephew of Kansas City political boss Tom Pendergast. With the support of Tom Pendergast, Truman won election after election. Truman was totally honest and his passion for honesty led him to national prominence when he chaired a U.S. Senate committee that uncovered egregious cost overruns, flagrant subpar quality and shady unethical dealings by numerous U.S. defense contractors during World War II.

Upon the death of FDR, Truman became president at one of the most challenging times in our country's history. Decisions to be made covered such monumental matters as post-war Germany, post-war ravished and starving Europe, Stalin, the Berlin Blockade and Airlift, the Bomb, Israel, MacArthur and the Korean War. This common Midwestern American man did his job admirably, with guts, confidence and without ego or pomp.

FAMILY BACKGROUND *and* INFLUENCES *on* TRUMAN'S CHARACTER

Harry S. Truman, generally of English ancestry, was born in the small town of Lamar, Missouri, in 1884 to John Anderson Truman and Martha Young Truman. John was a fairly successful farmer and livestock trader. Mother Martha came from a family of Confederate sympathizers whose farm was ravaged by Union troops. She was direct, frank and outspoken. Harry was the oldest child of three siblings. Harry later in life frequently commented that he had a happy childhood. He was always neat and clean, a "mama's boy" and said,

"To tell the truth, I was kind of a sissy."[3]

Harry and his mother remained close throughout her life. Martha lived to see her son through his first two years as president.

When Harry was six, the family moved to a farm outside Independence, Missouri. About this time Harry started wearing thick glasses and his doctor told him not to compete in contact sports. Harry took piano lessons which he enjoyed and he practiced every day. He also was an avid reader, especially of history. In high school he also helped out by working before and after school at a local drugstore.

Harry graduated from high school in 1901 and shortly thereafter his father went bankrupt from trading grain futures. There was no money to send Harry to college so Harry found work in various clerical positions, and then later worked on the family farm.

In 1917 at age thirty-three Harry went off to artillery training at Fort Sill, Oklahoma. At Fort Sill he helped run the camp store. He also became friends with James Pendergast, nephew of Tom Pendergast, the "boss" of the Kansas City Democratic party political machine.

Harry was promoted to captain and put in charge of Battery D, 129th Field Artillery. They were shipped to France and Harry took with him six pairs of glasses. He came home somewhat of a war hero. His war experiences transformed his life, for Harry learned he had courage under fire and learned that he possessed leadership skills. He also learned to play poker, which he played almost daily throughout his life.

After the war, Harry opened a men's clothing store in Kansas City with a friend, with whom he ran the Fort Sill camp store. The store was initially successful but failed in 1921. With encouragement from his army buddy James Pendergast, Harry decided on a career in politics and ran to be a county commissioner. He won the election in 1922, lost in 1924, but won again in 1926 and 1930.

Shortly after his return from World War I, Harry married Elizabeth "Bess" Wallace (1885-1982). They had been friends since childhood. Bess was Harry's first and only love. She was from a wealthy family, was athletic and a tomboy. Bess's mother never thought Harry was good enough for Bess and Harry and his mother-in-law had a difficult relationship. When Bess was age eighteen her father shockingly committed suicide.

Harry and Bess had one daughter, Mary Margaret (1925-2008), who graduated from George Washington University in 1946 and became a classical soprano singer and an author.

In 1934 Truman was elected to the U.S. Senate and reelected in 1940. In the interim, in 1939 Tom Pendergast went to prison for tax evasion.

Upon Pendergast's death, Truman attended the funeral. Truman when asked to comment by reporters said,

"You don't forget a friend."[4]

Truman was placed on the national ticket as vice president with Franklin Roosevelt in 1944. Roosevelt died April 12, 1945 when Truman had been vice president for only a couple of months. Roosevelt had ignored Truman and Truman knew little of the issues confronting the nation then at war in Europe and the Pacific.

CHARACTER PROFESSOR TRUMAN'S RED WHITE *and* BLUE CHARACTER GEMS

Truman's Character Gem No. 1

APPRECIATE AND CELEBRATE THE COMMON EVERYDAY AMERICAN VALUES OF WORK HARD, DO YOUR BEST, AND HAVE UNQUESTIONABLE INTEGRITY AND DECENCY.

Truman could be described as a common, ordinary man. David McCullough in his book *Truman* writes:

"He stood for common sense, common decency. He spoke the common tongue. As much as any President since Lincoln, he brought to the highest office the language and values of the common American people. He held to the old guidelines: work hard, do your best, speak the truth, assume no airs, trust in God, have no fear. Yet he was not and had never been a simple, ordinary man."[5]

Truman's Character Gem No. 2

THE BUCK STOPS HERE! DON'T AVOID MAKING A DECISION.

Truman understood his job was to timely make decisions and so the plaque on his desk read

"The Buck Stops Here"

He made momentous decisions while president. He had no qualms about accepting responsibility for his decisions.

He told biographer Merle Miller,

"...it isn't the strong men that have caused us most of the trouble, it's the ones who were weak...the ones who just sat on their asses and twiddled their thumbs..."[6]

Truman's Character Gem No. 3
DO THE BEST YOU CAN AND THEN DON'T BE A WORRIER.

Once a decision was made, Truman had no regrets and didn't worry about it.

Lyndon Johnson observed,

"...the great thing about Truman is that once he makes up his mind about something – anything...he never looks back and asks, 'Should I have done it?'...he just knows he made up his mind as best he could and that's that."[7]

Truman's Character Gem No. 4
LEARN TO ACCEPT CRITICISM BUT, "IF YOU CAN'T STAND THE HEAT, YOU BETTER GET OUT OF THE KITCHEN".

Truman could make decisions because he could cope with criticism that he knew would be forthcoming from somewhere. He commented,

"No one who accomplished things could expect to avoid mistakes.

Only those who did nothing made no mistakes."[8]

In 1946 he told his wife,

"I'm doing as I damn please for the next two years and to hell with them all."[9]

Truman's Character Gem No. 5
DON'T MAKE A DECISION BASED ON WHAT IS POPULAR WITH OTHERS.

Besides not worrying about criticism because he could "take the heat", he also was willing to make unpopular decisions. He was comfortable with his own values and principles.

"I wonder how far Moses would have gone, if he had taken a poll in Egypt."[10]

When Truman fired General Douglas MacArthur, MacArthur was one of the most popular Americans.

In a 1973 article from Time magazine, Truman was quoted as saying in the early 1960's:

"I fired him because he wouldn't respect the authority of the President. I didn't fire him because he was a dumb son of a bitch, although he was, but that's not against the law for generals. If it was, half to three-quarters of them would be in jail."[11]

Truman's Character Gem No. 6
A HAPPY FAMILY LIFE IS GOAL NUMBER ONE.

To Truman the most significant event in his life was his marriage to Bess. Although they married late (thirty-five and thirty-four years old respectively), they were married for fifty-three years. Bess and daughter Margaret were the core foundation of his life. His vitality, his ability to cope with stress and his overall health benefited from his family life.

Truman's Character Gem No. 7
WORK HARD, FIGHT AND "GIVE 'EM HELL".

"Give 'em Hell Harry" was a fighter, who is said to have worked twice as hard as most presidents. Of course, a good example is the election in 1948 when no one gave him a chance of victory. He crisscrossed the nation by train, traveling some 30,000 miles to win over Thomas Dewey. Clark Clifford commented on Truman's fight for reelection,

"It wasn't in my opinion he was a skilled politician that he won. He was a good politician…a sensible politician…But that wasn't why he was elected President…It was the remarkable courage in the man – his refusal to be discouraged, his willingness to go through the suffering of that campaign, the fatigue, the will to fight every step of the way, the will to win…It wasn't Harry Truman the politician who won, it was Harry Truman the man."[12]

Truman,

"It takes work to do anything well. Most people expect everything and do nothing to get it. That is why some people are leaders in

society, in politics, in religion, on the stage and elsewhere, and some just stand and cry that they haven't been treated fairly."[13]

A reporter noted that,

"…in a fight, this quiet man can and does hurl devastating fire…"[14]

A colleague had this view,

"One tough son-of-a-bitch of a man."[15]

Truman's Character Gem No. 8
TWO HEADS ARE BETTER THAN ONE.

Truman didn't feel threatened by folks who might be smarter or have more experience on some topics.

Truman's Character Gem No. 9
IT IS OKAY TO DISLIKE SNOBS.

Truman disdained snobbery and pretense, folks he called "high hats".

"There were more prima donnas per square foot in public life in Washington than in all the opera companies ever to exist."[16]

Harry was totally humble,

"I tried never to forget who I was, and where I came from, and where I would go back to."[17]

Truman's Character Gem No. 10
DON'T BE A MONEY GRUBBER.

Truman disdained those who chase the almighty dollar at the expense of honor and integrity. He advised folks not to ruin their life chasing money and envying those with more.

Truman's Character Gem No. 11
BE A PEOPLE PERSON!

Truman was a people person. He legitimately liked people, liked meeting them and liked talking to them, which brought enjoyment to him in his everyday life. He didn't try to mislead or manipulate people, which distinguished him from many of his predecessors.

He felt all people were basically good, until he sometimes learned otherwise. Kansas City reporter William Helm,

"Truman regarded every man as a gentleman until he showed up as another package."[18]

He was loyal to his friends and his friends and colleagues and they returned this loyalty to him. One long time White House staff member commented that Truman,

"liked people, he trusted people, and in turn he engendered a feeling of unqualified loyalty and devotion among his staff."[19]

Truman's Character Gem No. 12
IT IS OKAY TO NOT HAVE MUCH INTEREST IN THEORY OR ABSTRACT IDEAS.

Truman dealt only with the here and now.

Truman's Character Gem No. 13
BE AT ALL TIMES, NEAT AND CLEAN.

Truman from a young age was repeatedly described as neat and clean. As an adult he wore snappy bow ties.

Truman's Character Gem No. 14
JOIN THE ARMED FORCES AND RESTART YOUR LIFE.

For Truman, joining the Armed Forces was a positive life changing event. He gained confidence, was cool and calm under fire, and learned he could be a leader.

Truman's Charater Gem No. 15
CULTIVATE AND ENJOY HOBBIES.

Truman's principal activity was spending time with his wife and daughter. He also enjoyed nightly "poker with the boys", playing the piano and classical music.

Eisenhower while President, 1956

CHAPTER FOURTEEN

PERSONAL CHARACTER VALUES OF PRESIDENT AND CHARACTER PROFESSOR DWIGHT D. EISENHOWER
(1890-1969)
(34th U.S. President 1953-1961)

SUPERB LEADERSHIP COMBINING the "EISENHOWER GRIN" with an "IRON FIST IN A VELVET GLOVE"

"...the popularity of President Eisenhower has got beyond the bounds of reasonable calculation and will have to be put down as a national phenomenon, like baseball. The thing is no longer just a remarkable fact but kind of national love affair..."[1]

—JAMES RESTON
in *The New York Times*, 1955

"Ben Hogan for President. If we're going to have a golfer, let's have a good one."[2]

—Bumper Sticker during the 1956 election campaign

Ike speaking to paratroopers of the 101st Airborne Division on D-Day, June 5, 1944

Eisenhower landing a fish after WWII and before presidency, 1946

Ike with "The King" Arnold Palmer

"I Like Ike" was more than a campaign slogan. People legitimately liked Eisenhower and Eisenhower legitimately liked people. He was simply a "good guy" and folks wanted to work with him or for him or just in some way be his friend. He was picked by FDR to be Commander-In-Chief of the Allied Forces and in charge of the D-Day assault not because he was a great military strategist, but because he had a reputation of being able to successfully bring together diverse personalities and diverse self-interests to work together as a team.

However those who knew him intimately knew that behind his famous grin, was a tough competitor and a tough taskmaster with a serious temper. He had an "Iron Fist in a Velvet Glove".

FAMILY BACKGROUND *and* INFLUENCES *on* EISENHOWER

Dwight D. Eisenhower was born in 1890 in Denton, Texas, and moved in 1892 to Abilene, Kansas, which he always considered his hometown. He was the third of seven sons. Eisenhower had a strong religious, lower middle class upbringing. His father, David Jacob Eisenhower, was of Pennsylvania Dutch ancestry and his mother, Ida Stover Eisenhower, of German Protestant ancestry. Both were rigid disciplinarians and his father regularly used physical punishment. Roughhousing amongst brothers was a daily occurrence. Bible reading took place every evening. Both parents were pacifists, especially his mother. Eisenhower as a youth was active with hunting, fishing, cooking, sports (especially football and baseball), card playing, reading western novels and books on military history. After high school he could not afford the cost of college so he worked for a couple of years in a dairy creamery before being accepted to West Point. At West Point Eisenhower was a better athlete than student. He was a star running back on the varsity football team until a knee injury ended his career during his sophomore year. Football remained important to Eisenhower. Eisenhower would coach football from time to time at schools near the posts to which he was then assigned.

After West Point Eisenhower was initially assigned to San Antonio, Texas where he met and married nineteen year old Mamie Doud, a wealthy debutante from Colorado.

Ike and Mamie had two sons, Doug "Icky" Eisenhower (1917-1921) who died from scarlet fever at age three, and John Eisenhower (1922-2013) who went to West Point, had a successful career in the Army and later became Ambassador to Belgium.

As was normal for West Point graduates, the Eisenhowers constantly were moving from one Army post to another. During World War I Eisenhower, to his chagrin, was stateside training tank crews.

To his benefit Eisenhower was recognized for his organizational and administrative skills. He was selected to attend a U.S. Army Command and General Staff College where he graduated first in his class of 245. This led Eisenhower away from a career of commanding troops but rather toward a career on the administrative staffs of various Generals, including Douglas MacArthur, John Pershing, George C. Marshall and William Moseley.

MacArthur once wrote of Eisenhower,

*"This is the best officer in the U.S. Army. When the next war comes, move him right to the top."*³

Eisenhower once wrote of MacArthur,

*"Yes, I knew [General MacArthur] well. Very well, indeed. I studied dramatics under him for years."*⁴

Perhaps due to Eisenhower's organizational skills, his career dramatically changed during World War II when at age fifty-two he received his first troop command as Supreme Commander of the Allied Forces in North Africa for Operation Torch. Subsequently he was named Supreme Commander of all Allied Forces, including being in charge of Project Overlord, the D-Day Allied invasion of France.

After the war, Eisenhower served two years as president of Columbia University, a position in which he was not comfortable, and two years as Supreme Commander of NATO. He easily was elected U.S. president in 1952 and reelected in 1956. He had health problems during his presidency including a serious heart attack in 1955 and a stroke in 1957.

CHARACTER PROFESSOR EISENHOWER'S RED WHITE *and* BLUE CHARACTER GEMS

Eisenhower's Character Gem No. 1

KEEP PLUGGING AWAY; PREPARE AND BE READY WHEN YOUR NUMBER IS CALLED AND IT'S YOUR TURN TO SHINE.

Eisenhower's career for the first thirty years consisted exclusively of administrative staff positions. He had accomplished nothing remarkable and he was extremely frustrated, but like a back-up football quarterback, tried to be positive, be prepared and ready if he ever got his big chance.

"Whenever I had convinced myself that my superiors, through bureaucratic oversight and insistence on tradition, had doomed me to run of the mill assignments, I found no better cure than to blow off steam in private and then settle down to the job at hand."[5]

When discussing his less than spectacular career…

"the real satisfaction was for a man who did the best he could. My ambition in the Army was to make everybody I worked for regretful when I was ordered [transferred] to other duty."[6]

He kept plugging away in administrative roles, pleasing his superiors, and then late in his career, at age fifty-two, he "came off the bench" and his opportunity came.

Eisenhower's Character Gem No. 2
LOVE LIFE AND PEOPLE.

Stephen E. Ambrose, a recent biographer of Eisenhower, has written about Eisenhower's personal character values,

"…and most of all a love of life and of people…Eisenhower loved life and he loved people. To me that is the heart of Eisenhower's character. From it flowed all the rest."[7]

Eisenhower's Character Gem No. 3
BE A "GOOD GUY"!

Eisenhower's military success and his political success were both in large part due to his personal nature. He was friendly, sociable and tactful and people wanted to work for him or be his friend.

British Field Marshall Montgomery on Eisenhower:

"His real strength lies in his human qualities. He has the power of drawing the hearts of men as a magnet attracts the bit of metal. He merely has to smile at you and you trust him at once."[8]

Lyndon Johnson:

"The sturdy and enduring virtues – honor, courage, integrity, decency, all found expression in the life of this good man and noble leader."[9]

Eisenhower's Character Gem No. 4
NO NEED TO BE THE CENTER OF ATTENTION.

Eisenhower was humble and never needed to be the center of attention and liked to say,

"Always take your job seriously, never yourself."[10]

"I'm just folks, I come from the people, ordinary people."[11]

Eisenhower's Character Gem No. 5
ASSOCIATE WITH SMART PEOPLE.

Eisenhower:

"Always try to associate yourself with and learn as much as you can from those who know more than you do, who do better than you, who see more clearly than you."[12]

Eisenhower's Character Gem No. 6
FIND WORK-LIFE BALANCE.

Work a 36 hole golf work-week.

Eisenhower's Character Gem No. 7
STAY CALM AND DON'T OVERREACT.

Eisenhower knew that patience could be a virtue and frequently advised others,

"Make no mistake in a hurry."[13]

His calmness was a stabilizing force at times of stress.

Eisenhower's Character Gem No. 8
TEAMWORK BRINGS SUCCESS.

Teamwork was the primary reason for Ike's success. Eisenhower knew the importance of "team". He played and coached football at West Point, and later coached high school and college football for a total of ten years as he transferred from Army post to Army post.

"I believe that football, perhaps more than any other sport, tends to instill in men the feeling that victory comes through hard – almost slavish – work, team play, self- confidence and an enthusiasm that amounts to dedication."[14]

Lessons learned from football led to being selected as the Supreme Allied Commander in Europe, which eventually led to becoming president. As Supreme Allied Commander he had to overcome national pride and rivalries and meld into a successful team the air, sea and ground military forces of American, British and French troops.

General Lucius Clay:

"General Eisenhower was remarkably gifted in bringing people from a variety of backgrounds together and forging then into a successful team."[15]

Eisenhower's Character Gem No. 9
POWER OF CLEAR AND CONCISE ARTICULATION.

Eisenhower learned the benefit of articulating clearly and concisely. This skill was recognized by several of his superiors.

General George Moseley:

"You possess one of those exceptional minds…always drawing sound conclusions and, equally important, you have the ability to express those conclusions in clear and convincing form."[16]

Eisenhower's Character Gem No. 10
ATTAIN SUCCESS BY FRIENDLY PERSUASION AND BUILDING MORALE.

"You don't lead by hitting people over the head; that's assault, not leadership."[17]

To boost morale, he would be optimistic, he would be enthusiastic, he would listen to criticisms, he would be fair in his judgments and not prejudicial. He knew optimism is infectious.

Eisenhower's Character Gem No. 11
CONTROL YOUR TEMPER AND DON'T LET CRITICISM OR DISAGREEMENTS GET THE BEST OF YOU.

Eisenhower successfully kept his temper in check.

Eisenhower's Character Gem No. 12
HAVE AN IRON FIST IN A VELVET GLOVE.

"I like Ike", the iconic phrase used in the 1952 and 1956 elections was true for so many Americans, including colleagues and staff. At West Point one cadet comments,

"Everyone liked him and apparently he liked everyone in turn."[18]

General Omar Bradley:

"Ike liked people and it is awfully hard for them not to like him in return."[19]

However, inside him a fire burned, he had a hot temper, was extremely competitive and could be harsh, blunt and demanding. He expected his orders to be followed to the letter. General Lucius Clay, a close friend and colleague:

"General Eisenhower was not the easiest person in the world to work for…and if you did not measure up, you were gone. He had no tolerance for failure."[20]

Perhaps the paperweight prominently displayed on his desk summarizes it best:

"Gently in manner, strong in deed."[21]

Eisenhower's Character Gem No. 13

APPRECIATE THE IMPORTANCE OF PLANNING, ORGANIZATIONAL AND ADMINISTRATIVE WORK.

Eisenhower's spectacular career was the result of his organizational skills and attention to details. While his superiors were getting the glory, Eisenhower was in the backroom doing the planning and paperwork.

Eisenhower's Character Gem No. 14

BE STRONGLY AGAINST WAR.

"I hate war as only a soldier who has lived it can, only as one who has seen its brutality, its futility, its stupidity."[22]

"Our most valued, our mostly costly asset is our young men. Let's don't use them any more than we have to."[23]

Eisenhower's policy while president was there would be no limited wars, no involvement in foreign conflicts. He avoided sending troops to Vietnam, Suez and Formosa, amongst others.

"What separates me from the pacifists is that I hate the Nazis more than I hate war."[24]

Eisenhower's Character Gem No. 15
CULTIVATE AND ENJOY HOBBIES.

Eisenhower's passion was golf. He also enjoyed poker and bridge (highly skilled), oil painting (landscapes and portraits), fishing, football and reading western novels.

*Ford receiving from Caroline Kennedy and Ted Kennedy
the Kennedy Profiles in Courage Award for pardoning Nixon*

CHAPTER FIFTEEN

PERSONAL CHARACTER VALUES OF PRESIDENT AND CHARACTER PROFESSOR GERALD R. FORD
(1913-2006)
(38th U.S. President 1974-1977)

A CLEAN-CUT ALL AMERICAN BOY *who* BECAME PRESIDENT BECAUSE *of* HIS INTEGRITY *and* TRUSTWORTHINESS

"God has been good to America, especially during difficult times. At the time of the Civil War, he gave us Abraham Lincoln, and at the time of Watergate, he gave us Gerald Ford – the right man at the right time who was able to put our nation back together again."[1]

—TIP O'NEILL,
political adversary of Republican Ford when Democratic Speaker of the House

"Gerald Ford was our only President to be a normal human being."[2]

—HENRY KISSINGER

"I doubt if there has ever before been a time when integrity has so surpassed ideology in the judging of a man for so high an office."[3]

—ALLEN CRANSTON,
Democratic U.S. Senator, California, supporting Republican Ford

Ford with wife Betty watching the losing election returns, November 1976

Raised in America's Heartland in a tight knit middle class family, Gerald Ford was an Eagle Scout at age 15, attended church every Sunday, consistently worked odd jobs to earn needed money, was a star collegiate athlete, a *Cosmopolitan* magazine cover model, a Yale law graduate and a World War II naval officer with ten battle stars, all of which led George H.W. Bush to call him,

"a Norman Rockwell painting come to life."[4]

When Spiro Agnew resigned as vice president in shame for accepting bribes, Ford was picked to replace him because of his integrity and trustworthiness, knowing that he might soon replace Nixon as president as a result of the then on-going Watergate investigations. James Cannon, a White House aide to Ford and later a Ford biographer, recounts,

"Ford was honest. He could be trusted…Ford had proved himself to be a man of integrity. It was for that integrity that the highest powers of Congress, Democratic and Republican, chose Ford to be Vice President, knowing that Nixon's presidency was doomed."[5]

So we already have our first Ford Character Gem – "Integrity", but there are more to come from this "Rockwell painting come to life".

FAMILY BACKGROUND *and* INFLUENCES *on* FORD'S CHARACTER

Gerald Ford was born in Omaha, Nebraska in 1913 with the name Leslie Lynch King, Jr. His biological father, of English ancestry and considerable wealth, physically abused Ford's mother, Dorothy Gardner King. Dorothy fled with her baby Gerald back to her parents then living in Grand Rapids, Michigan, which at that time was one of the furniture manufacturing capitals of the U.S. Dorothy King met Gerald R. Ford, Sr., a paint salesman, at an Episcopalian church social and the couple were married in 1917. The couple had three sons of their own, and Gerald R. Ford, Sr. officially adopted young Jerry. Gerald Sr. was moderately successful in the paint business, but during the Depression, the Fords lost their home.

Young Jerry was active in the Boy Scouts, his church, swimming at the YMCA, and waiting tables and doing odd jobs to help out financially. His main passion was competitive sports, participating in football, basketball and track. He attended the University of Michigan to play football, but had to continue to wait tables to help pay his way. After college he turned down several contract offers to play professional football and instead went to Yale to become an assistant football coach so he could go to Yale Law School. He dated a New York City fashion model and their photo appeared on the cover of *Cosmopolitan*. *Look* magazine did a spread of seventeen photos. Shortly after he graduated from Yale Law School, World War II broke out and Ford spent four years as a Naval officer including two years in the Pacific, earning numerous battle stars.

After the war, Ford returned to Grand Rapids to practice law. In 1948 he ran for Congress and in the Republican primary defeated the incumbent. Shortly before the general election Ford, at age thirty-four, married Betty Bloomer (1918-2011), an attractive and vivacious fashion coordinator, ex-model and dancer with the well-known Martha Graham Dance Company. They had three sons and one daughter.

Betty was an activist for the Equal Rights Amendment, pro-choice, and a leader in the "Women's Movement". In 1974 she had a mastectomy and went public, speaking out to raise awareness of breast cancer. She also went public about her battle with alcoholism and substance abuse. She was the first Chair of the Board of Directors of the Betty Ford Center for Rehabilitation.

HEAR YE! HEAR YE!

CHARACTER PROFESSOR FORD'S RED WHITE *and* BLUE CHARACTER GEMS

Ford's Character Gem No. 1

THE ROAD TO HAPPINESS AND SUCCESS STARTS WITH THE FUNDAMENTAL HUMAN VALUES OF INTEGRITY, HONESTY AND DECENCY.

Ford was both literally and figuratively an Eagle Scout, and proud of it. He was proud of his Midwest humble background, proud of his hardworking parents, his churchgoing, his competitive team sports. Ford wrote,

"It is the quality of the ordinary, the straight, the square, that accounts for the great stability and success of our nation. It is a quality to be proud of. But it's a quality that many people seem to have neglected."[6]

Tom DeFrank, a reporter for Newsweek, wrote,

"Jerry Ford is a human being cum laude, a down-to-earth, earnest, genuine likeable guy with an infectious laugh and not the slightest hint of pretentiousness...Jerry Ford sticks out as a man of abundant decency."[7]

Ford's Character Gem No. 2

QUALITY PARENTING: THE IMPORTANCE OF THE ROLE OF BEING A PARENT.

James Cannon, his White House aide and biographer, places prime importance on Ford's parents and his upbringing:

"The qualities of character that placed Ford in the White House and guided his decisions as President run like golden threads to his childhood, leading back to a time and place and family that instilled in the boy the integrity, loyalty, courage, stamina, ambition, patriotism, idealism, and the habit of hard work that became part of his being."[8]

Ford's Character Gem No. 3

BE PASSIONATE ABOUT TELLING THE TRUTH ALWAYS. IT MADE FORD U.S. PRESIDENT!

Ford was extremely passionate about truthfulness. His stepfather taught him,

"You are a person of your word. Rich or poor, famous or insignificant, the integrity of your word, your veracity, is a tremendous possession of great value. Keep it. Never lose it."[9]

Unlike several of the presidents that preceded Ford, Ford felt,

"I do not think a President under any circumstances that I can envision ought to lie to the American people."[10]

As Ford's fellow Congresswoman Martha Griffiths pointed out,

"In all the years I sat in the House, I never knew Mr. Ford to make a dishonest statement nor a statement part true and part false. He never attempted to shade a statement, and I never heard him utter an unkind word."[11]

Ford's Character Gem No. 4

VALUABLE LESSONS SUCH AS DISCIPLINE, PREPARATION, TEAMWORK AND GOOD SPORTMANSHIP ARE LEARNED FROM COMPETITIVE SPORTS.

Ford repeatedly gave credit to the lessons he learned from competitive team sports in high school and college. As his biographer Douglas Brinkley points out,

"Discipline, preparation, teamwork and adherence to a game plan may be the platitudes of the locker room but Ford carried them onto the political field."[12]

Ford said,

"Sports taught you how to compete but always by the rules, how to be part of a team, how to win, how to lose and come back and try again."[13]

For Ford, football was far more than just a game.

"I learned discipline", he said in later life. "I learned you were part of a team, especially as lineman, where you worked in the trenches with six other linemen. I learned to have a good attitude – it's infectious and can bring victory. I learned that losing a game was terrible, but you had to go on, prepare for the next game, and the next. I admired my coach. He inspired us. He motivated us. He taught us: 'You play to win. You give it everything you've got, but you always play within the rules'. We believed that. That's the way we played then. I still do."[14]

Character Professor Gerald R. Ford

Ford's Character Gem No. 5

THERE IS NO SUBSTITUTE IN LIFE FOR A HAPPY, LOVING FAMILY, AND UNDERSTAND THAT BEING A GOOD MOTHER IS THE MOST CHALLENGING JOB ON EARTH.

Ford and wife Betty were married for fifty-seven years until Ford's death. They were as loving and as close as a couple can be. Jerry respected his wife's outspoken views, even when they differed from his. Together they raised four children to adulthood.

Ford,

"There are no substitutes for father, mother and children bound together in a loving commitment to nurture and protect. No government, no matter how well intentioned, can take the place of the family in the scheme of things"[15],

and

"...there is no undertaking more challenging, no responsibility more awesome, than that of being a mother."[16]

Ford's Character Gem No. 6

DON'T BE A SHOW-OFF! BE A WORK HORSE, NOT A SHOW HORSE.

Upon assuming the Vice Presidency in 1973, Ford promptly showed his humility by telling the nation that he is "a Ford, not a Lincoln". His biographers describe him as a "work horse, not a show horse". When making a speech he regularly included some self-deprecating humor:

"I know I am getting better at golf because I am hitting fewer spectators."[17]

"I had pro offers from the Detroit Lions and Green Bay Packers…if I had gone into professional football, the name Jerry Ford might have been a household name today."[18]

Ford's Character Gem No. 7
WORK LIKE HELL!

Ford's father instilled Ford with the life concept that the harder you work, the luckier you are. Ford, looking back,

"And whether it was in such things as the Boy Scouts or athletics or academics, I worked like hell."[19]

Ford's Character Gem No. 8
KNOW YOURSELF, LIKE YOURSELF AND YOU WILL STOP BEING A WORRIER.

Betty remarked that even on most stressful days, Jerry would go to sleep immediately when his head was on the pillow.

Henry Kissinger remarked,

"Ford's inner peace was precisely what the nation needed."[20]

Cannon observed,

"He knew his reach and he knew his limits. He liked being Jerry Ford. He was at peace with himself."[21]

Ford's Character Gem No. 9

COOPERATE AND COMPROMISE WITH OTHERS WHENEVER POSSIBLE. LIVE TO FIGHT ANOTHER DAY.

Ford was in Congress for twenty-five years, rising to Republican Minority Leader. It was an era in which it was standard operating procedure for legislation to be the result of both political parties working together and compromising for the welfare of the nation. Today it seems "compromise" between our political parties is a lost art. Ford took this spirit of compromise to the White House and initiated various compromise programs, such as allowing Vietnam War draft dodgers to "earn" their amnesty through two years of alternative services.

His leadership style was not to be vindictive.

"That's counterproductive, he insisted. That person knows he has disappointed you. To rub it in makes it, the next time, literally impossible to get his cooperation. You can lose one battle, but the most important thing is to win the war."[22]

Ford's Character Gem No. 10
IT IS INSULTING TO YOUR COLLEAGUES NOT TO BE PUNCTUAL.

Growing up, the Ford family had three rules:

"Tell the truth, work hard, and come to dinner on time." [23]

Ford became a stickler with arriving on time, of managing time, and not wasting time. In high school, he had to juggle his studies, his three sports (football, basketball and track) and his part-time jobs (lawn mowing, waiting tables at a café across from his high school, etc.). At Yale, he had his law studies and his coaching jobs (and, of course, he had his New York City model girlfriend!).

Cannon writes,

"Quintessentially punctual, Ford believed a visitor's most precious asset, and his own, was time." [24]

Ford's Character Gem No. 11
PUBLIC SERVICE IS AN HONORABLE PROFESSION.

Ford was clearly not driven by ego, or the desire to accumulate wealth, contrary to several of his predecessors. Ford never accumulated any wealth during his 29 years of public service. He put the interests of his constituents and the nation ahead of any ethically questionable personal ambitions.

Character Professor Gerald R. Ford

Ford:

"I believe that a President has to exemplify by his personal life, the standards — morally, ethically and otherwise — by which most Americans live their lives." 25

Ford's Character Gem No. 12
CULTIVATE AND ENJOY HOBBIES.

Ford enjoyed golf, skiing (but stopped after having both knees replaced), daily exercise, college football (he even attended a game on the first day of his honeymoon), bridge, tennis, church, stamp collecting and his pet golden retriever Liberty.

Ford with Queen Elizabeth, 1976

CHAPTER SIXTEEN

PERSONAL REFLECTIONS

We have finished our exploration for advice from our fifteen American "Character Professors". I still worry about the strong trend toward ideological polarization, i.e. selecting leaders solely on ideology and neglecting personal character values in "this time of demoralization", as discussed in the Prologue. However this journey has put me in a much more positive frame of mind. I have been reinvigorated by our American heritage, culture and values. Thanks to these fifteen Professors we have collected a giant stash of Red White and Blue Character Gems. Plus during my research, I have possibly found a couple of excellent role models for my Character Mount Rushmore.

Each of the fifteen men possess numerous positive character values. In addition these men were not shy or defensive about letting the world know of these values. All spoke and/or wrote about their personal values. Franklin published his Thirteen Values for all to read and adopt. Most all of them wrote memoirs, even Silent Cal Coolidge, each of which provides insight into their personal character values.

Totally subjective on my part, the following are some of my favorite Red White and Blue Character Gems:

Franklin's Gem No. 2
SMILE, PUT A TWINKLE IN YOUR EYE.

Washington's Gem No. 3
YOU ARE DEFINED BY YOUR INTEGRITY AND YOUR MORAL AND ETHICAL STANDARDS.

Washington's Gem No. 10
VOLUNTEER, GIVE BACK TO THE COMMUNITY.

Adams' Gem No. 2
FIGHT FOR WHAT'S RIGHT! BE YOUR OWN PERSON, STUBBORNLY DEFEND YOUR OPINIONS AND DON'T WORRY ABOUT BEING "POPULAR".

Jefferson's Gem No. 10
EDUCATION IS THE CORNERSTONE OF PERSONAL HAPPINESS AND THE CORNERSTONE OF A HARMONIOUS SOCIETY.

Lincoln's Gem No. 2
KNOW YOURSELF! BE INTROSPECTIVE AND SELF-AWARE OF YOUR STRENGTHS AND WEAKNESSES.

Grant's Gem No. 5
QUIET DIGNITY! BE HUMBLE, BE LOW KEY, BE A "REGULAR GUY" WITHOUT PRETENSIONS.

Personal Reflections

Theodore Roosevelt's Gem No. 1
LIVE EVERY DAY TO ITS UTMOST
WITH THROTTLE WIDE OPEN.

Theodore Roosevelt's Gem No. 7
LEARN ABOUT AND ENJOY NATURE
AND THE GREAT OUTDOORS.

Coolidge's Gem No. 3
LIFE IS NOT JUST ABOUT HAVING A GOOD
TIME, BUT RATHER EVERY AMERICAN
HAS A DUTY TO HELP OTHERS.

Coolidge's Gem No. 4
REDUCE STRESS BY SIMPLY
DOING THE RIGHT THING.

FDR's Gem No. 1
STOP COMPLAINING!

FDR's Gem No. 2
NEVER GIVE UP. HAVE GUTS AND
DETERMINATION TO OVERCOME ANY
PHYSICAL HANDICAPS, SETBACKS OR DESPAIR.

Truman's Gem No. 5
DON'T MAKE A DECISION BASED ON
WHAT IS POPULAR WITH OTHERS.

Eisenhower's Gem No. 6
FIND WORK-LIFE BALANCE. WORK
A 36 HOLE GOLF WORK-WEEK.

Ford's Gem No. 4
VALUABLE LESSONS SUCH AS DISCIPLINE,
PREPARATION, TEAMWORK AND GOOD
SPORTSMANSHIP ARE LEARNED
FROM COMPETITIVE SPORTS.

AND A FEW MORE RED WHITE AND BLUE
CHARACTER GEMS RELATING TO FAMILY:

Adam's Gem No. 1
A SPOUSE BRINGS HAPPINESS AND IS THE
FOUNDATION FOR ALL ELSE IN LIFE.

Jefferson's Gem No. 7
APPRECIATE AND LOVE YOUR HOME.

TR's Gem No. 8
ENJOY FAMILY. "THE BEST CROP
IS THE CROP OF CHILDREN."

Wilson's Gem No. 4
ALLOW CHILDREN TO HAVE A CHILDHOOD.

Ford's Gem No. 5
THERE IS NO SUBSTITUTE IN LIFE FOR A
HAPPY, LOVING FAMILY, AND UNDERSTAND
THAT BEING A GOOD MOTHER IS THE MOST
CHALLENGING JOB ON EARTH.

HERE ARE A FEW OF MY FAVORITE QUOTES:

Franklin:
"Wine is the constant proof that God loves us and wants to see us happy."

Franklin:
"I would rather have it said, he lived usefully, than he died rich."

Franklin:
"Be at war with your vices, at peace with your neighbors, and let every new year find you a better man."

Franklin:
"More is to be learned with the ear than the tongue."

Adams:
When someone would complement Adams on the career of his son, John Quincy Adams, he often would reply, *"My son had a mother."*

Friend Jesse W. Fell on Lincoln:
"If there were any traits of character that stood out in bold relief, in the person of Mr. Lincoln, it was that of Truth, and Candor. He was utterly incapable of insincerity…In the grand review of his peculiar characteristics, nothing creates such an impressive effect as his love of the truth."

Lincoln:
"Always bear in mind that your own resolution to succeed is more important than any other one thing."

Lincoln commenting on Grant:
"…he has the grit of a bulldog. Once let him get his teeth in, and nothing can shake him off."

Comment about Theodore Roosevelt:
"Death had to take him sleeping, for if Roosevelt had been awake, there would have been a fight."

Theodore Roosevelt:
"It is surprising how much reading a man can do in time usually wasted."

Theodore Roosevelt:
"It is not the critic who counts, not the man who points out how the strong man stumbles, or where the doer of deeds could have done better. The credit belongs to the man who is actually in the arena, whose face is marred by dust and sweat and blood; who strives valiantly; who errs, and comes short again and again, because there is not effort without error and shortcoming; but who does actually strive to do the deeds; who knows the great enthusiasms, the great devotions; who spends himself in a worthy cause."

Theodore Roosevelt:
"I like to drink the wine of life with brandy in it."

A journalist on Coolidge:
"… people liked him because he kept his word and was scrupulously honest. He inherited from his Vermont ancestors their characteristics of plain living and high thinking, taciturnity and humor."

Hoover:
"There is one Congressman who is proof of a negative I.Q."

Hoover:
"Fishing is much more than fish. It is the great occasion when we return to the fine simplicity of our forefathers."

Wife Eleanor on FDR:
"Remember, the nicest men in the world are those who always keep something of the little boy in them."

Truman:
"It takes work to do anything well. Most people expect everything and do nothing to get it. That is why some people are leaders in society, in politics, in religion, on the stage and elsewhere, and some just stand and cry that they haven't been treated fairly."

Eisenhower:
"Always try to associate yourself with and learn as much as you can from those who know more than you do, who do better than you, who see more clearly than you."

Ford:
"It is the quality of the ordinary, the straight, the square, that accounts for the great stability and success of our nation. It is a quality to be proud of. But it's a quality that many people seem to have neglected."

Ford:
"I do not think a President under any circumstances that I can envision ought to lie to the American people."

HEAR YE! HEAR YE!

SELECTION OF MY CHARACTER ROLE MODELS

In conjunction with my search for Red White and Blue Character Gems, I selected four Character Professors for my personal Character Mount Rushmore.

Abe Lincoln
Simply said, a great human being. He may have been our most sensitive and humane president. He knew poverty, hardship and emotional despair, but through introspective reflection he was able to know himself which led to inner strength, humility and empathy for others. Of course he was truly "Honest Abe" which brought him success and respect as a trial lawyer and carried him all the way to the White House.

Ben Franklin
What a man and what a life! Franklin's personal character values brought him success, success and more success. He was self-made, rags to riches through hard work, frugality and kindness. He believed America was the land of opportunity. Significantly he cared about both (i) improving his own personal character values, and (ii) improving the quality of life for everyone in his community through his inventions, civic projects and governmental service. With a smile for all and a twinkle in his eye he lived a contented life, filled with friendships and accolades.

Gerald Ford
"A Norman Rockwell painting came to life."
Ford humbly told the nation he was "a Ford and not a

Lincoln", and while he may not have been Lincoln's equal, he still is one of my character role models. He was proud of his middle class upbringing, and the lessons learned from his parents. Because Ford told the truth and had unwavering integrity he was chosen to be vice president and then became president. While president,

"I believe that a President has to exemplify by his personal life, the standards – morally, ethically and otherwise – by which most Americans live their lives."

His life story says it all – Character Counts!

Harry Truman

Truman's persona when he was president was that he was an average man, a common man who was in the right place at the right time rising to become U.S. president. Today we know he was anything but average. He faced and made the most momentous decisions of any president. The "buck" did stop with Harry and he dealt with it. He was able to cope with stress because he had rock solid character values. He knew a happy family life was goal number one. He liked people and his "poker with the boys". He had humility even after becoming president.

"I never tried to forget who I was, and where I came from, and where I would go back to."

HEAR YE! HEAR YE!

OF COURSE MOST READERS MAY DIFFER FROM MY SELECTIONS WHEN CHOOSING THEIR PERSONAL RED WHITE AND BLUE CHARACTER ROLE MODELS.

1. George Washington
A man of resolute unimpeachable integrity who made great sacrifices for the good of others.

2. John Adams
A true patriot who argued and fought for what he believed was right and didn't worry about being popular. He was a man of total honesty and virtue. John and Abigail had a true love affair and appreciated that family was the cornerstone of happiness.

3. Thomas Jefferson
A man of ideas and ideals who believed education is priority number one. He was quiet, polite to all and avoided in-person confrontations. He dressed casually and avoided pomp and ceremony. He was completely open to change, and believed a previous generation shouldn't overly bind the next generation.

4. Ulysses S. Grant
Courageous military man, yet also a gentle and loving family man who conducted himself in an understated non-egotistical manner. Late in life through persistence and strength of character, he overcame earlier failure and humiliation. Because he knew hardship, he always showed respect and compassion for others. The epitaph on his tomb reads *"Let us have peace."*

5. Theodore Roosevelt

One of our country's hardest working and most successful presidents.

"I like to drink the wine of life with brandy in it."

He loved life and lived every minute to its utmost. He fought tenaciously up San Juan Hill, then to regulate powerful monopolies and to protect America's park lands.

6. William Howard Taft

A congressman remarked about President Taft,

"No one, it seemed, was immune to his wholesome, warmhearted, genial charm and modest gentle character – he was probably the most likeable man to ever hold the Office of the President."

7. Woodrow Wilson

A man who was driven to do great deeds for the benefit of others.

8. Calvin Coolidge

An extremely popular president who brought to the White House his New England and Puritan temperament that all Americans have a duty to help others. He was president during the Roaring 20's but believed,

"Prosperity is only an instrument to be used, not a deity to be worshipped."

9. Herbert Hoover

Called the Great Humanitarian, Hoover rose from a poor orphan to a successful, independently wealthy mining executive through hard work and determination. He retired from his business endeavors at a young age and devoted the remainder of his life to public service.

10. Franklin Roosevelt

With guts and determination he struggled to lead a normal life despite being paralyzed from the waist down. He found much success, and Winston Churchill called him the greatest man he had ever known. He was both a lion and a fox.

11. Dwight Eisenhower

Ike's personal character values allowed him to adroitly blend being a "good guy" with being a strong leader who was uniformly respected and admired by his colleagues. As British Field Marshall Bernard Montgomery said about Ike, *"His real strength lies in his human qualities."*

NOTES

ALL SOURCES ARE SECONDARY SOURCES

PROLOGUE
1. Robert Dallek, *Preface to Franklin D. Roosevelt: A Political Life* (Penguin Books, 2017)
2. Robert Dallek, *Preface to Franklin D. Roosevelt: A Political Life* (Penguin Books, 2017)
3. Bill Moyers, *10 Big Fat Lies and the Liars Who Told Them; billmoyers.com* (June 27, 2014)
4. Bill Moyers, *10 Big Fat Lies and the Liars Who Told Them; billmoyers.com* (June 27, 2014)
5. Bill Moyers, *10 Big Fat Lies and the Liars Who Told Them; billmoyers.com* (June 27, 2014)
6. Bill Moyers, *10 Big Fat Lies and the Liars Who Told Them; billmoyers.com* (June 27, 2014)
7. *Clinton Accused, What Clinton Said;* washingtonpost.com
8. National Public Radio, Read Trump's January 6 Speech, A Key Part of Impeachment Trial; npr.org (February 10, 2021)
9. The Lehrman Institute, *Mr. Lincoln & Friends; The Lawyers:* Jesse W. Fell; Mrlincoln and friends.org
10. James Cannon, *Gerald R. Ford: An Honorable Life*, page 144 (The University of Michigan Press, 2013)

CHAPTER ONE: BENJAMIN FRANKLIN

PRINCIPAL SOURCES
WI]   Walter Isaacson, *Benjamin Franklin: An American Life* (Simon & Schuster Paperbacks, 2004)

[GSW]   Gordon S. Wood, *The Americanization of Benjamin Franklin* (The Penguin Press, 2003)

NOTES

1. *Benjamin Franklin Quotes*; Goodreads.com
2. WI, page 127
3. WI, page 481
4. *Benjamin Franklin Quotes*; Goodreads.com
5. Alli Page, 9 *Successful Characteristics Embodied by Ben Franklin*; Lifeback.org
6. *Benjamin Franklin Quotes*; Goodreads.com
7. WI, pages 89-90
8. GSW, page 233
9. *Benjamin Franklin Quotes*; Goodreads.com
10. WI, page 99
11. *Benjamin Franklin Quotes*; Goodreads.com
12. *Benjamin Franklin Quotes*; Goodreads.com
13. *Benjamin Franklin Quotes*; Goodreads.com
14. WI, page 56
15. M.S. Rao, *Benjamin Franklin's Greatest Soft Skills*; profmsr.blogspot.com
16. WI, page 4
17. WI, page 349
18. M.S. Rao, *Benjamin Franklin's Greatest Soft Skills*; profmsr.blogspot.com
19. WI, page 102
20. *Benjamin Franklin Quotes*; Goodreads.com
21. WI, page 104
22. GSW, page 234
23. *Benjamin Franklin Quotes*; Goodreads.com
24. *Benjamin Franklin Wine Quotes*; WineIntro.com
25. M.S. Rao, *Benjamin Franklin's Greatest Soft Skills*; profmsr.blogspot.com

CHAPTER TWO: GEORGE WASHINGTON

PRINCIPAL SOURCES

[RC] Ron Chernow, *Washington: A Life* (Penguin Books, 2011)
[JE] Joseph J. Ellis, *His Excellency* (First Vintage Books Edition, 2005)
[PCL] Steven J. Rubenzer and Thomas R. Faschingbauer, *Personality, Character & Leadership in the White House* (Potomac Books, Inc., 2004)

NOTES

1. RC, page 766
2. JE, page 73
3. RC, page 13
4. JE, page 272
5. RC, page 394
6. Jeff Dacus, *George Washington Character Lessons*, page 4, georgewashingtonmythsymbolandreality.org (Boston University, 2005)
7. Jeff Dacus, *George Washington Character Lessons*, page 4, georgewashingtonmythsymbolandreality.org (Boston University, 2005)
8. Jeff Dacus, *George Washington Character Lessons*, page 6, georgewashingtonmythsymbolandreality.org (Boston University, 2005)
9. RC, page 186
10. PCL, page 276
11. PCL, page 270
12. Jeff Dacus, *George Washington Character Lessons*, page 7, georgewashingtonmythsymbolandreality.org (Boston University, 2005)
13. RC, page 370
14. RC, pages 457-8
15. Gordon S. Wood, *The Greatness of George Washington* (The Virginia Quarterly Review, Volume 68, Spring 1992)
16. Jeff Dacus, *George Washington Character Lessons*, page 5, georgewashingtonmythsymbolandreality.org (Boston University, 2005)

CHAPTER THREE: JOHN ADAMS

PRINCIPAL SOURCES

[DM]   David McCullough, *John Adams* (Simon & Schuster Paperbacks, 2001)

[GSW]   Gordon S. Wood, *Friends Divided: John Adams and Thomas Jefferson* (Penguin Press, 2017)

NOTES

1. DM, page 163
2. GSW, page 134
3. DM, page 262

4. DM, page 479
5. DM, page 626
6. DM, page 373
7. *Quotes, John Adams Historical Society*; John-Adams-heritage.com
8. DM, page 207
9. *Quotes, John Adams Historical Society*; John-Adams-heritage.com
10. DM, page 373
11. DM, page 33
12. DM, page 590
13. *John Adams Quotes,* Goodreads.com
14. GSW, pages 43-44
15. Steven J. Rubenzer and Thomas R. Faschingbauer, *Personality, Character & Leadership in the White House,* page 124 (*Potomac Books, Inc., 2004*)
16. GSW, page 106
17. DM, page 127
18. DM, page 238
19. DM, page 609
20. GSW, page 429
21. DM, page 415

CHAPTER FOUR: THOMAS JEFFERSON

PRINCIPAL SOURCES

[JM]   Jon Meacham, *Thomas Jefferson: The Art of Power* (Random House Trade Paperback Edition, 2013

[JJE]   Joseph J. Ellis, *American Sphinx: The Character of Thomas Jefferson* (First Vintage Edition, 1998)

[GSW]   Gordon S. Wood, *Friends Divided: John Adams and Thomas Jefferson* (Penguin Press, 2017

NOTES

1. JM, page 501
2. Kathryn Gehred, *The Washington Papers* (University of Virginia); washingtonpapers.org
3. Steven J. Rubenzer and Thomas R. Faschingbauer, *Personality,*

Character & Leadership in the White House, page 124 (*Potomac Books, Inc., 2004*)
4. JM, page 308
5. JJE, page 44
6. GSW, page 245
7. Robert Dallek, *Hail to the Chief*, page 51 (Oxford University Press, 1996)
8. JM, page 224
9. GSW, page 104
10. JM, page 504

CHAPTER FIVE: ABRAHAM LINCOLN

PRINCIPAL SOURCES

[DKG]   Doris Kearns Goodwin, *Team of Rivals* (Simon & Schuster Paperbacks, 2005)

[DHD]   David Herbert Donald, *Lincoln* (Simon & Schuster Paperbacks, 1995)

NOTES

1. DKG, page 724
2. DHD, page 19
3. DKG, page 449
4. DKG, page 54
5. The Lehrman Institute, *Lincoln & Churchill*; (Lincolnandchurchill.org/personality – leadership)
6. Stephanie Chu, *Abraham Lincoln as a Leader*; (Prezi.com)
7. DKG, page 104
8. Lincoln's Second Inaugural Address, nps.gov
9. DKG, page 103
10. The Lehrman Institute, *Abraham Lincoln's Classroom*, page 52.
11. The Lehrman Institute, *Mr. Lincoln & Friends*; *The Lawyers*, Jesse W. Fell; Mrlincolnfriends.org
12. The Lehrman Institute, *Mr. Lincoln & Friends*; *The Lawyers*, William H. Herndon; Mrlincolnfriends.org
13. DHD, page 149

14. DKG, page 165
15. DKG, page 680
16. DKG, page 502
17. DHD, page 270
18. DHD, page 270
19. DKG, page 748

CHAPTER SIX: ULYSSES S. GRANT

PRINCIPAL SOURCES

[RC]   Ron Chernow, *Grant* (Penguin Press, 2017)
[JES]   Jean Edward Smith, *Grant* (Simon & Schuster Paperbacks, 2001)
[WSM]   William S. McFeely, *Grant* (Norton Paperbacks, 1982)
[PCL]   Steven J. Rubenzer and Thomas R. Faschingbauer, *Personality, Character & Leadership in the White House* (Potomac Books, Inc., 2004)

NOTES

1. RC, page IX
2. JES, page 92
3. RC, XXIII
4. RC, page 122
5. RC, page 297
6. RC, page 384
7. WSM, page 27
8. *Grant the Family Man, Ulysses S. Grant Homepage*; www.granthomepage.com
9. RC, page 96
10. JES, page 15
11. JES, page 14
12. JES, page 98
13. RC, page XX
14. RC, page XX
15. RC, page 11
16. *Ulysses S. Grant, Up Close and Personal*; The College of St. Scholastica; libguide.css.edu/usgrant/home/upclose
17. RC, page XXII

18. RC, page XXII
19. JES, page 457
20. RC, page XXI

CHAPTER SEVEN: THEODORE ROOSEVELT

PRINCIPAL SOURCES

[EM]   Edmund Morris, *Theodore Rex* (Random House Trade Paperbacks, 2010)

[MOH]   David McCullough, *Mornings on Horseback* (Simon & Schuster Paperbacks, 2003)

[DKG]   Doris Kearns Goodwin, *The Bully Pulpit* (Simon & Schuster Paperbacks, 2014)

[PCL]   Steven J. Rubenezer and Thomas R. Faschingbauer, *Personality, Character & Leadership in the White House* (Potomac Books, Inc., 2004)

NOTES

1. DKG, page 681
2. EM, page 30
3. EM, page 451
4. DKG, page 5
5. Quotes.thefamouspeople.com
6. MOH, page 160
7. MOH, page 160
8. MOH, page 207
9. MOH, page 160
10. MOH, page 160
11. EM, page 15
12. PCL, page 237
13. DKG, page 81
14. MOH, page 330
15. PCL, page 243
16. PCL, page 239
17. DKG, page 68
18. EM, pages 6-7
19. EM, page 420

20. MOH, page 275
21. DKG, page 746
22. Robert Dalleck, *Hail to the Chief*, page 138 (Oxford University Press, 1996)
23. DKG, page 723
24. Edmund Morris, *Theodore Roosevelt, President*; Americanheritage.com, Volume 32, Issue 4, June/July 1981
25. PCL, page 244
26. DKG, page 111
27. DKG, page 40
28. DKG, page 40
29. DKG, page 231
30. DM, page 224
31. MOH, page 340
32. DKG, page 232
33. DKG, page 67
34. DKG, page 76
35. PCL, page 237
36. DKG, page 47
37. PCL, page 246

CHAPTER EIGHT: WILLIAM HOWARD TAFT

PRINCIPAL SOURCES

[DKG]   Doris Kearns Goodwin, *The Bully Pulpit* (Simon & Schuster Paperbacks, 2013)

[JA]   Judith I. Anderson, *William Howard Taft; Buckeye Presidents* (Philip Weeks, Editor; The Kent State University Press, 2003) (Kindle Edition)

[LG]   Lewis L. Gould, *The William Howard Taft Presidency* (University Press of Kansas, 2009)

NOTES

1. JA, page 231
2. JA, page 212
3. DKG, page 51

4. DKG, page 430
5. JA, page 213
6. JA, page 212-213
7. DKG, page 136
8. DKG, page 146
9. DKG, page 539
10. DKG, page 390
11. DKG, page 395
12. JA, page 222
13. JA, page 224

CHAPTER NINE: WOODROW WILSON

PRINCIPAL SOURCES

[WWCH] Alexander L. George and Juliette L. George, *Woodrow Wilson and Colonel House, A Personality Study* (Plunkett Lake Press, 2017)

[HWB] H.W. Brands, *Woodrow Wilson* (St. Martins Press, 2003)

[JC] John Milton Cooper, Jr., *Woodrow Wilson* (First Vintage Books Edition, 2011)

[PCL] Steven J. Rubenzer and Thomas R. Faschingbauer, *Personality, Character & Leadership in the White House* (Potomac Books, Inc., 2004)

NOTES

1. WWCH, page XX
2. PCL, page 133
3. WWCH, page 8
4. HWB, page 25
5. PCL, page 132
6. WWCH, page 135
7. PCL, page 127
8. HWB, page 28
9. HWB, page 9

CHAPTER TEN: CALVIN COOLIDGE

PRINCIPLE SOURCES

[RS]   Robert Sobel, *Coolidge: An American Enigma* (Recent History 2015) (Paperback)

[RHF]   Robert H. Ferrell, *The Presidency of Calvin Coolidge* (University Press of Kansas, 1998)

[AS]   Amity Shlaes, *Coolidge* (Harper Perennial, 2013) (Paperback)

[DG]   David Greenbert, *Calvin Coolidge* (Timebooks, Henry Holt and Company, 2006)

NOTES

1. William Allen White, *A Puritan in Babylon; The Story of Calvin Coolidge* (Simon Publications, 2001)
2. RS, pages 133-134
3. RS, page 161
4. RS, page 18
5. RS, page 418
6. DG, page 15
7. RS, page 24
8. *The New York Times Obituary*, January 6, 1933
9. *The New York Times Obituary*, January 6, 1933
10. RS, pages 235-236
11. RS, page 138
12. DG, page 8
13. RS, page 55
14. RS, page 18
15. RHF, page 24
16. RS, page 18
17. RHF, page 205
18. *Quotations, Calvin Coolidge Presidential Foundation*; coolidgefoundation.org
19. RS, page 86
20. RS, page 120
21. RHF, page 13
22. DG, page 60
23. RS, page 134
24. RS, page 19
25. RHF, page 198
26. RS, page 26
27. *Quotations, Calvin Coolidge Presidential Foundation*; coolidgefoundation.org

28. AS, page 314
29. *The New York Times Obituary*, January 6, 1933
30. RS, page 137
31. RS, pages 157-158
32. Z. Hereford, *The Power of Persistence*; essentiallifeskills.net
33. *Calvin Coolidge Quotes*; brainyquote.com

CHAPTER ELEVEN: HERBERT HOOVER

PRINCIPAL SOURCES

[CR]   Charles Rappleye, *Herbert Hoover in the White House, The Ordeal of the Presidency* (Simon & Schuster Paperbacks, 2017)

[GJ]   Glen Jeansonne, *Herbert Hoover: A Life* (New American Library, Penguin Random House LLC, 2016)

NOTES

1. David Frum, *Herbert Hoover is the Model Republicans Need* (The Atlantic, November 26, 2017)
2. Herbert Hoover Quotes; brainyquote.com
3. GJ, page 23
4. CR, page 67
5. CR, page 69
6. GJ, page 105
7. CR, page 17
8. Herbert Hoover; goodreads.com
9. *The New York Times Obituary* (McCandlish Phillips, October 21, 1964)

CHAPTER TWELVE: FRANKLIN DELANO ROOSEVELT

PRINCIPAL SOURCES

[HWB]   H.W. Brands, *Traitor To His Class* (First Anchor Books Edition, 2009)

[JES]   Jean Edward Smith, *FDR* (Random House Trade Paperbooks, 2008)

[DKG]   Doris Kearns Goodwin, *No Ordinary Time* (Simon & Schuster Paperbacks, 1994)

NOTES

1. JES, page XI
2. HWB, page 824
3. HWB, page 594
4. HWB, page 158
5. JES, page 211
6. HWB, page 87
7. Doris Kearns Goodwin, *Character Above All*, page 22 (Simon & Schuster, 1995)
8. Doris Kearns Goodwin, *Character Above All*, page 18 (Simon & Schuster, 1995)
9. JES, page 238
10. JES, page 315
11. HWB, page 128
12. HWB, page 630
13. DKG, page 203
14. JES, page 298
15. HWB, page 241
16. Doris Kearns Goodwin, *Character Above All*, page 17 (Simon & Schuster, 1995)
17. Smith, page XI
18. DKG, page 199

CHAPTER THIRTEEN: HARRY S. TRUMAN

PRINCIPAL SOURCES

[DMCC] David McCullough, *Truman* (Simon & Schuster Paperbacks, 1992)

[RHF] Robert H. Ferrell, *Harry S. Truman: A Life* (University of Missouri Press, 1994)

[PCL] Steven J. Rubenzer and Thomas R. Faschingbauer, *Personality, Character & Leadership in the White House* (Potomac Books, Inc., 2004)

[BYU] Blake E. Adams, *President Truman's Personality and Leadership*; Sigma: Journal of Political and International Studies, Volume 5, Article 6, 1987 (BYU Scholar Archive) [CAA] David McCullough, *Harry S. Truman; Character Above All* (Robert A. Wilson, Editor; Simon & Schuster, 1995)

NOTES

1. DMCC, page 525
2. DMCC, page 989-990
3. DMCC, page 45
4. CAA, page 53
5. DMCC, page 991
6. BYU, page 86
7. BYU, page 89
8. DMCC, page 467
9. CAA, page 40
10. CAA, page 52
11. "Historical Notes: Giving Them More Hell" (Time Magazine, December 3, 1973)
12. DMCC, pages 717-718
13. RHF, page 134
14. DMCC, page 208
15. PCL, page 189
16. DMCC, page 467
17. PCC, page 194
18. RHF, page 370
19. DMCC, page 556

CHAPTER FOURTEEN: DWIGHT D. EISENHOWER

PRINCIPAL SOURCES

[JES] Jean Edward Smith, *Eisenhower in War and Peace* (Random House Trade Paperback Edition, 2013)

[SEA] Stephen E. Ambrose, *Dwight D. Eisenhower; Character Above All* (Robert A. Wilson, Editor; Simon & Schuster, 1995)

[PCL] Steven J. Rubenzer and Thomas R. Faschingbauer, *Personality, Character & Leadership in the White House* (Potomac Books, Inc., 2004)

NOTES

1. JES, page 670
2. JES, page 581
3. *The Presidents Fact Book*, page 557 (Black Dog & Leventhal, 2016)
4. *The Presidents Fact Book*, page 557 (Black Dog & Leventhal, 2016)
5. JES, page 42
6. SEA, page 66
7. SEA, page 61
8. SEA, page 63
9. PCL, page 147
10. SEA, page 66
11. JES, page 3
12. Brent Bauer, *Seven Business Leadership Lessons from Dwight Eisenhower* (Forbes Leadership Forum, January, 2017)
13. SEA, page 78
14. JES, page 25
15. JES, page 551
16. JES, page 93
17. Brent Bauer, *Seven Business Leadership Lessons from Dwight Eisenhower* (Forbes Leadership Forum, January, 2017)
18. JES, page 25
19. JES, page 26
20. JES, page 180
21. Brent Bauer, *Seven Business Leadership Lessons from Dwight Eisenhower* (Forbes Leadership Forum, January, 2017)
22. JES, page IX
23. JES, page 635
24. SEA, page 64

CHAPTER FIFTEEN: GERALD R. FORD

PRINCIPAL SOURCES

[JC]   James Cannon, *Gerald R. Ford: An Honorable Life* (The University of Michigan Press, 2013)

[DB]   Douglas Brinkley, *Gerald R. Ford* (Time Books, Henry Holt and Company, LLC, 2007)

Notes

[CAA] James Cannon, *Gerald R. Ford; Character Above All* (Robert A. Wilson, Editor; Simon & Schuster, 1995)

[PCL] Steven J. Rubenzer and Thomas R. Faschingbauer, *Personality, Character & Leadership* (Potomac Books, Inc., 2004)

NOTES

1. JC, page 462
2. JC, page VII
3. DB, pages 53-54
4. President George H.W. Bush's Eulogy for President Ford (Gerald R. Ford Presidential Library & Museum, January 2, 2007; fordlibrarymuseum.gov)
5. CAA, page 147
6. Time Magazine, August 29, 1974
7. JC, page 165
8. CAA, page 147
9. JC, page 83
10. JC, page 144
11. PCL, page 154
12. DB, page 5
13. JC, page 43
14. JC, page 48
15. Gerald R. Ford Quotes; brainyquote.com
16. Presidential Proclamation (March 5, 1976; fordlibrarymuseum.gov)
17. Gerald R. Ford Quotes; goodreads.com
18. Gerald R. Ford Quotes; brainyquote.com
19. The New York Times Obituary (James M. Naughton and Adam Clymer, December 27, 2006)
20. JC, page 11
21. JC, page 332
22. The New York Times Obituary (James M. Naughton and Adam Clymer, December 27, 2006)
23. CAA, page 149
24. JC, page 332
25. JC, page 147

ILLUSTRATION LIST AND CREDITS

Prologue — Eisenhower, Patton and Truman in Berlin 1945; U. S. Army, Harry S. Truman Presidential Library

Taft and T. Roosevelt at Taft's Inaugural 1909; Harris & Ewing Collection, Library of Congress

Chapter 1 — Ben Franklin, painting by Joseph Siffred Duplessis, 1783; National Portrait Gallery, Smithsonian Institution

Chapter 2 — George Washington, painting by Rembrandt Peale, 1795; National Portrait Gallery, Smithsonian Institution

George Washington in Uniform of Colonel in Virginia Militia, painting by Charles Willson Peale, 1772; Washington – Curtis Lee Collection, Washington and Lee University

Chapter 3 — John Adams, painting by Gilbert Stuart, between 1800-1815; National Gallery of Art

Abagail Adams, painting by Benjamin Blyth, 1766; Massachusetts Historical Society

Chapter 4 — Thomas Jefferson, painting by Rembrandt Peale; White House Collection/White House Historical Association

Thomas Jefferson, John Adams and Benjamin Franklin editing the Declaration of Independence, painting by Jean Leon Gerome Ferris, 1776; Virginia Museum of History & Culture

Chapter 5 — Abraham Lincoln and son Tad, engraving by Brady Studio, 1868; Library of Congress

Lincoln at Antietam Maryland, 1862; Library of Congress

HEAR YE! HEAR YE!

Chapter 6   Ulysses S. Grant, painting by Thomas Le Clear, 1880; National Portrait Gallery, Smithsonian Institution

Grant at Cold Harbor Virginia, 1864; Library of Congress

Chapter 7   Theodore Roosevelt "Big Smile" when in the Amazon after his presidency, 1910; Library of Congress

Theodore Roosevelt with silver-mounted Bowie knife from Tiffany's while in the Badlands, 1885; credit Wikimedia Commons

Colonel Roosevelt of the Rough Riders, photo by George Gardner Rockwood, 1898; Library of Congress

Theodore Roosevelt with wife Edith and their six children, 1903; Library of Congress

Roosevelt with John Muir; Welcome Collection, Attribution 4.0 International

Chapter 8   William Howard Taft, painting by Anders Leonard Zorn, 1911; The White House Historical Association

William Howard Taft playing golf at Seattle Golf Club, 1909; University of Washington, Museum of History and Industry

Chapter 9   Woodrow Wilson, painting by Frank Graham Cootes, 1913; The White House Historical Collection

Chapter 10   Calvin Coolidge with wife Grace (nicknamed "Sunshine") and dog Prudence Prim, 1924; Library of Congress

Coolidge with the great Walter Johnson, 1925; Library of Congress

Chapter 11   Herbert Hoover with his dog King Tut, 1928; Library of Congress

Hoover fishing 1929; National Photo Company Collection, Library of Congress

Chapter 12   Franklin Roosevelt at Yalta Summit, 1945 with Churchill and Stalin; U.S. National Archives, Army Signal Corps Collection

240

Illustration List and Credits

Eleanor Roosevelt with the Universal Declaration of Human Rights, 1949; FDR Presidential Library & Museum, Photo ID 57697

Franklin Roosevelt with wife Eleanor and children Anna and James, 1908; FDR Presidential Library & Museum

Chapter 13   Harry S. Truman; Harry S. Truman Presidential Library

President Truman with General MacArthur, 1950; Harry S. Truman Presidential Library

Truman with wife Bess and daughter Margaret, 1934; Roger Reynolds, Harry S. Truman Presidential Library

Chapter 14   President Eisenhower, 1956; Dwight D. Eisenhower Presidential Library, Museum & Boyhood Home

Eisenhower speaks with paratroopers of the 101st Airborne Division just before Normandy invasion, June 5, 1944; Dwight D. Eisenhower Presidential Library, Museum & Boyhood Home

Eisenhower landing a fish, 1946 after WWII and before the presidency; State Library and Archives of Florida, flickr.com/photos/floridamemory

Ike with "The King" Arnold Palmer 1960; Smithsonian Magazine, September 16, 2016 (photo by Paul Vathis, Associated Press)

Chapter 15   Ford receiving the Kennedy Profiles in Courage Award; John F. Kennedy Presidential Library and Museum, Boston.

President Ford with wife Betty watching the losing election returns, November 1976; White House Photograph Courtesy Gerald R. Ford Library

President Ford with Queen Elizabeth, 1976; White House Photograph Courtesy Gerald R. Ford Library

Chapter 16   Three cartoons by Dave Granlund, cartoonist; www.davegranlund.com

ABOUT THE AUTHOR

Jim Tervo was raised in Michigan, including attending the University of Michigan for both undergrad (Phi Beta Kappa) and law school. Jim's initial law career focused on banking and real estate, with stints in Detroit, then Chicago where Jim met and married Janet Burch and then San Francisco. Starting in 2002 his focus was international financial transactions and Jim and Janet spent ten excellent years in Asia, first in Tokyo, then in Shanghai and then in Hong Kong.

In retirement at The Sea Ranch in Sonoma County California, Jim began arising every morning around 5 am to read copious number of pages on American history, especially excellent biographies of our past presidents by such esteemed authors as Walter Isaacson, Ron Chernow, David McCullough and Doris Kearns Goodwin to name but a few. He was impressed by many of the presidents' thoughts on character and felt everyone could benefit from a reflection on their advice.

Janet assisted on all aspects of this book.

www.ingramcontent.com/pod-product-compliance
Lightning Source LLC
Chambersburg PA
CBHW041455010526
44107CB00014B/1050